Let Equity Prevail

Prevail

Recollections And Reflections

Lord Nicholls of Birkenhead

Published by D & M Heritage Press

Dunn & Mills Business Park
Red Doles Lane
Huddersfield
West Yorkshire
HD2 1YE

First published 2015

ISBN: 978-1-911148-01-2

Author's note:
By courtesy, the aerial photograph of Birkenhead School
comes from the pictorial history of the school published
by the Old Birkonian Society; the photographs of the
ruins of Birkenhead Priory, Woodchurch Road School
and the war damage to St Saviour's church from *Yesterday's
Wirral* published by Ian and Marilyn Boumphrey; and the
photograph of offices at Port Sunlight from *Liverpool 800*
published by Liverpool University Press. I am also indebted
to *Birkenhead at War 1939–45* by Ian Boumphrey for air raid
dates and statistics.

I am particularly grateful to my son-in-law Dr Stephen
Christie for his invaluable and unfailing help with technical
computer problems I encountered from time to time when
producing the typescript for this book.

To Jenny
To Whose Love and Support
I Owe So Much

Contents

EARLY YEARS

1. *By The River*   3
    New Ferry: January 1933

2. *Wartime*   9
    Prenton in the Blitz: December 1939

3. *Birkenhead School*   21
    Noctorum: September 1943

FIRST JOBS

4. *Introduction To Law*   31
    Port Sunlight: September 1949

5. *The Meerut Photograph*   35
    National service: April 1951

UNIVERSITIES

6. *Learning The Law*   43
    Heswall and Liverpool: 1953

7. *Learning More Law*   49
    Cambridge: October 1956

8. *Bar Finals – The Last Exams*   55
    Cornwall: spring 1958

AT THE BAR

9. *Wearing A Wig*   59
    Starting at the Bar: November 1958

10. *Marriage*   65
     King Henry's Road: August 1960

11. *By Another River*   67
     Stoke D'Abernon: autumn 1962

12. *On The Hill*   71
     Cobham: February 1969

13. *Making Progress*   73
     A red bag

14. *A Longer Wig*   77
     Silk: Easter 1974

ON THE BENCH

15. *Red Robes And A Different Wig*   83
     High Court bench: October 1983

16. *Black And Gold Robes*   91
     Court of Appeal: February 1986

17. *Still Black And Gold*   99
     Vice-Chancellor: October 1991

18. *Best Bib And Tucker*   105
     Ceremonial occasions

19. *The Next Generation*   109
     Schools and weddings

20. *Change Of Venue*   115
     House of Lords: October 1994

21. *The Queen's Council*   125
     Judicial Committee: October 1994

22. *Not Always A Judge*   127
     Other commitments: 1996

23. *China*   129
     Hong Kong Court of Final Appeal: 1999

24. *Time To Change*   133
     Keeping the law up to date

25. *Not Always Right*   143
    Dissenting judgments

26. *Never Say Never*   149
    Decisions for tomorrow

27. *Travelling Again*   153
    More law abroad

28. *Middle Temple*   161
    Treasurer: 1997

29. *A Coat Of Arms*   167
    Let Equity Prevail: 1995

30. *The End Of The Law Lords*   171
    The new Supreme Court

COME OUT INTO THE SUN

31. *A Change Of Scene*   179
    Holidays

32. *Deus Nobis Haec Otia Fecit*   191
    In the garden

33. *Family*   197
    Past and present

34. *Time To Stop*   201
    Retirement: 2007

35. *Eighty Years*   203
    Cliveden: January 2013

36. *Looking Back*   207
    2015

Early Years

CHAPTER I

By The River
New Ferry: January 1933

I WAS ALMOST sixty years old when I first saw a photograph of my mother. I had recently been appointed as vice-chancellor after serving as a judge in the Court of Appeal for over six years.

I was born on 25th January 1933. Eleanor, my mother, suffered from tuberculosis and rheumatic arthritis and died from bronchopneumonia on 1st March 1939, aged forty-three. I was six and my brother Clifford was nearly eight years old.

We were both born in Tilstock Avenue in New Ferry, Bebington, on the Wirral. This was an unexciting cul-de-sac sandwiched between the river Mersey and the New Chester Road. We lived in a modest semi-detached house built in the 1920s. As young boys Clifford and I walked a few hundred yards to Dell School, an infants' school in a dell abutting directly onto the river. I must have been very little, because every afternoon I had a sleep on the school floor on a blanket.

Schools were different then. On one occasion the headmistress called us into her room because another boy had been bullying Clifford. She made each of us solemnly give him a punch. An interesting form of discipline.

Every day at exactly 1pm we heard the 'One O'Clock Gun' fired in Morpeth dock, triggered electronically from the Observatory on Bidston Hill, on the far side of Birkenhead. It provided an invaluable time signal to the maritime trade. Some days, depending on the wind, the bang startled the small birds and set them fluttering. The original cannon was a relic of the Crimean War and was first heard in September 1867.

Occasionally as we came home from school we bought Walls ice cream from a vendor ringing his bell as he pedalled a tricycle labelled 'Stop me and buy one'. In the daytime we saw the ships and the tugs way out on the river, and at night listened to the warning foghorns. There was always something happening on the river. It was the backdrop of our early life.

New Ferry was a misleading name for the district. The ferry service had come and gone before we were born, but the story behind this is interesting.

August 1934, aged 1 year 7 months with Clifford, at Tilstock Avenue.

It all arose from the unusual configuration of the river Mersey. Near the sea the river was about three-quarters of a mile across in its narrowest stretch. There a wooded headland jutted forward into the water. Further inland the river widened enormously, to three miles at its widest point. In the year 1150 Benedictine monks chose this headland as the site for their priory. The headland with its birch trees supplied the name Birkenhead. Here the monks set up a ferry to carry passengers from the Cheshire to the Lancashire side. This was the original ferry.

For many centuries little changed. Birkenhead remained a small rural village. After the dissolution of the monasteries in 1536 few people lived there. At the beginning of the 19th century the population was still barely one hundred souls, but its location beside the river was the foundation for its future prosperity. The original abbey was a sad ruin when I saw it as a boy at school. The birch trees had gone.

Meanwhile on the other side of this expanse of water Liverpool had grown apace, with money from the cotton trade and participation in the slave trade. This had not brought any benefit to the Wirral peninsula. The villages in Wirral were distanced from this industrial revolution by the physical barrier of the Mersey. Rowing across

Birkenhead Priory: remains of the Prior's Hall.

such a wide stretch of river would not have been attractive even on the calmest of days and even though the monks had done so for several centuries.

The catalyst for change was the coming of steam-powered ferryboats. Early in the 19th century steam ferries started across the river from Liverpool to Woodside and Tranmere. As these services became more reliable Wirral attracted the wealthier citizens of Liverpool, keen to escape from the ever expanding smoky confines of the city. The land was far cheaper, the air was cleaner, and the prospect of rural peace on the Wirral beckoned. The area was ripe for development, and Birkenhead grew into a flourishing town.

When growth came it was dramatic. Shipbuilding began in 1829. Thirty years later the town introduced the first horse-drawn tramway in Britain. By the end of the century the population had swollen to 110,000. The lane used by the monks to reach their farm known as The Grange became Grange Road, the principal shopping road in the town. Here, in the headquarters of the Birkenhead YMCA, Lord Baden-Powell held the inaugural meeting of the Boy Scout movement in 1908.

The Cammell Laird shipyards became renowned throughout the world, building many famous merchant vessels and warships. In 1938 Clifford and I witnessed from afar the launch of the Cunard liner RMS *Mauretania*. Warships included the aircraft carrier HMS *Ark Royal* and the battleship HMS *Prince of Wales*. Both ships played leading roles in World War II. The *Ark Royal* was renowned as a 'lucky ship' but ultimately its luck ran out in November 1941 when it was torpedoed by a German U-boat in the Mediterranean. The *Prince of Wales* was active in the defence of Singapore but was sunk off Malaya by Japanese air attacks in December 1941. This signalled the end of traditional battleships.

During the 19th century the Mersey ferry services expanded their reach to newly developing residential areas: downstream to New Brighton and Wallasey, upstream to the aptly named Rock Ferry and, even further, to New Ferry. In 1865 Mr Macfie, a sugar refiner from Liverpool, built at his own expense (£10,000) a new iron pier at New Ferry. But in the early hours of 30th January 1922 in a thick fog a Dutch ship, en route to Manchester, ran through his pier demolishing two spans. That put an end to the New Ferry service. It had lasted sixty years but passenger trade had declined. In 1886 a railway tunnel had been constructed under the river, and the Mersey Railway provided a speedier route to Liverpool. Reopening the ferry service was not worthwhile.

The New Ferry name continued to adhere to the locality, as also happened to the neighbouring settlement of Rock Ferry to the north.

My recollections of family life in Tilstock Avenue are few and simple: a tortoise in the garden, jumpers my mother had knitted, a revolving summerhouse for her to get some sunshine. I remember spilling a tin of white paint on the lawn and then covering it with grass cuttings.

Dad was a quiet and reserved man. After he remarried he thought it best, perhaps understandably, to destroy all records and reminders of those earlier years. He never talked of them. They must have held many desperately unhappy memories. It seems to have been accepted practice in those days that when a widower remarried photographs of the first spouse were put away and the children of the first marriage encouraged to accept the second wife as their 'mother'.

So, to this day, I know little about my mother beyond the formal facts recently unearthed from public records with the help of my niece Catherine and my nephew Tim. She was born in Salford, Lancashire, in 1895 and married my father in Birkenhead on 5th September 1929. She had qualified as a teacher in Stockwell, southwest London. Of her home and parents and childhood I am profoundly ignorant. I have just one clear recollection of her. She was scrubbing the kitchen

My father and mother on their wedding day.

floor and traced my name in the soapsuds. I do not recall her face or voice or anything she ever said. The few photographs I eventually saw came from a cousin of my mother. I only learned the date and cause of her death within the last couple of years.

CHAPTER 2

Wartime
Prenton in the Blitz: December 1939

MY FATHER WORKED in Lloyds Bank which he had joined at the age of fifteen on leaving school. It was there he met Mum, as Clifford and I always called her. She lived nearby in New Ferry and was the eldest of four daughters one of whom, Jessie, had learning difficulties. Their family home had been in Bidston, where their father was an insurance agent, collecting premiums from door to door, along the lines of the once-familiar 'man from the Pru'.

Both parents had died young. Mum was then twenty-one and Jean, the youngest daughter, was still at school aged twelve. So from an early age Mum shouldered the responsibility of her family, no easy task in any era. She worked in Liverpool at a jobcentre, then known as a labour exchange. Earlier, on leaving school, she had modelled clothes as a 'mannequin', a more dignified occupation in those days.

Britain entered the second world war on 3rd September 1939. I remember listening to the wireless and hearing Neville Chamberlain's announcement. The occasion is seared on my memory. Even to a young boy this was a tense and unforgettable moment. This news prompted Mum and Dad to bring forward their wedding plans and they married in December 1939. Dad was thirty-seven years of age and Mum thirty.

When he remarried my father moved house and set up a new home with Mum and us two boys in Prenton. This was three miles inland from the river and a better residential area than New Ferry. Like Bebington, Prenton was an old village swallowed up by Birkenhead as it expanded.

The only notable feature about Prenton was that, as with Bebington, it was one of the remarkable number of outlying villages spread around the Wirral whose names end with the syllable 'ton'. This was derived from the Anglo-Saxon 'tun', meaning town. Other examples are Barnston, Bidston, Burton, Claughton, Elton, Gayton, Hooton, Mollington, Moreton, Neston, Newton, Oxton, Poulton, Puddington, Storeton, Sutton, Thornton Hough, Thurstaston, Upton and Willaston. Most of them had developed residentially by the 1930s.

Our new home was a 1920s semi-detached house with four bedrooms. This remained the family home until 1952. For a short time a 'live in' maid used the smallest bedroom, known to us as 'the box room', but the war soon put an the end to that arrangement when she went off to work in a factory.

Much of this period was overshadowed by the war and its aftermath. A notable feature of World War II was its 'total war' character. Men were conscripted into the armed forces or to work down the coalmines as 'Bevin boys'. But homeland production of arms and food became essential. Women were mobilised to an unprecedented extent, after 1941 by conscription, into factories, armed forces and on the land ('the Women's Land Army'). In consequence the status of women changed permanently. Their role, and place, in society were never the same again. Not for the first time a major war brought about a major structural social change.

Identity cards were issued in October 1939. My identity number was LEGE 245-3. The number 3 showed I was the third member of the family, the other two being my father and elder brother. Restrictions and rationing were inevitable. At the outbreak of war Britain imported more than half of its food. Not surprisingly, the first commodity to be subject to restrictions, and that happened immediately, was petrol. We did not qualify for an allowance of petrol as this was strictly limited to priority users. So our four-door Morris Eight, with a three-speed gearbox and a handle for cranking the engine, was put on blocks in the garage 'for the duration' to save the tyres.

Individual ration books for food soon followed, and gradually food rationing became ever more wide-ranging and stringent. Clothing, also rationed, was produced in a 'utility' style with limits on the number of items such as pockets and buttons and pleats. Children who grew more quickly qualified for extra clothing coupons. For this purpose our feet were measured at school at regular intervals. To Mum's disappointment I never qualified.

Domestic coal was rationed, so were all kinds of soap. The size of newspapers was restricted, and wrapping paper for most goods was prohibited.

Fresh fruit and vegetables were not rationed, nor was fish. Cod was plentiful and cheap on Merseyside. Offal and game remained unrationed, but you had to smile sweetly at your butcher to obtain sausages or liver. Oranges and bananas were never seen. To satisfy children's craving for sweets greengrocers gave a raw carrot to any child who asked. Bread lost its whiteness through the use of more whole wheat but it was not rationed until after the war. This came about when the continual rain in mid-1946 ruined Britain's wheat crop. This wet summer was followed by an exceptionally long and cold winter. In Prenton snow lay on the ground for two months, from the end of January to the end of March 1947. Frost destroyed a huge amount of stored potatoes and potato rationing was introduced. Of this rationing I have no recollection, so it must have been fairly benign and short lived.

The egg ration was meagre: one egg per week, often less, supplemented by packets of dried eggs. We often went without. For some time we kept hens in the garden, with varying degrees of success. Feed for the hens was in lieu of our egg ration. We started by buying half-a-dozen day-old chicks. They all died, except for one tough little bird which turned out to be a cockerel. Clifford and I wore short trousers and it used to peck our ankles. As was to be expected in an urban area, when it started crowing the neighbours objected, so it had to go.

Unlike many people we were able to cope with the shortage of sugar. Our parents used sugar in their tea but we boys did not. So Mum was popular with neighbours, swapping our sugar for their margarine. With her baking and careful management we never went short. With gradually increasing allowances rationing continued for fifteen years until 1954 when, at last, meat eventually came off ration nine years after the end of the war.

House building stopped at the outbreak of war, to enable building materials to be reserved for the 'war effort'. This meant that part-completed houses, of which there were several in Prenton, stood open to the skies. These were irresistible play areas for trespassing schoolboys. As the war continued the number of these sites increased as one house after another was bombed and rendered uninhabitable. On one site I stumbled over the rubble and fell while carrying a broken roof slate to protect the seat of my bicycle from the rain. The ensuing gash through to the bone of my right leg left a scar visible to this day.

Careless Talk Costs Lives, Dig for Victory, Make-do and Mend, Holidays at Home were among the government's exhortations, plus the rhetorical question: Is your journey really necessary? These were meaningful to us, not just interesting slogans in a history book. We holidayed at home in 1940. Dad dug up the grass patches behind and in front of our house, and turned them into plots for potatoes and cabbages and sprouts.

Our principal source of news was the six o'clock bulletin on the wireless. To preclude the risk of misleading broadcasting the news readers always announced their names: 'this is the news read by (Alva Liddell) (Stuart Hibberd)'. Their voices became familiar.

As preparations for war gathered pace uniformed service personnel were increasingly seen on the streets. Contrast today, when for their own safety service men and women travel in mufti and change into uniform when they reach their depots and offices. After the USA entered the war long convoys of jeeps and larger vehicles wound slowly through Prenton on their way from the docks to a camp in Arrowe Park. In summer the American troops staged baseball matches in the nearby football stadium of Tranmere Rovers where I watched them several times. The Americans also took over the Wirral Ladies golf course, next to Birkenhead School's playing fields in Noctorum. Sometimes the troops gave the boys doughnuts and bottles of Coca-Cola, then a novelty in this country.

They all melted away in the spring of 1944 for the Allied D-Day landings on 6th June along a 50-mile stretch of the coast of Normandy. This was the largest seaborne invasion in history, with 5,000 ships carrying 200,000 soldiers. At home we listened avidly to every wireless bulletin, and I recorded their progress day-by-day by colouring the map of France in my school atlas. It was tremendously exciting. But that was all much later.

In 1940 the prospect of a German invasion was a real fear. The Wirral peninsula lies between two rivers, the Dee and the Mersey, and close to the Irish Sea. With its low-lying coastline, developed infrastructure and nearness to the Liverpool docks the area was peculiarly vulnerable. To make life more difficult for any invading force the signposts on all the roads were removed. Most of the side roads in Prenton were blocked off with barbed wire and hefty concrete blocks, in order to confine invaders to the main roads where machine gun posts ('pill boxes') had been constructed. The beaches were similarly protected, with additional landing obstacles.

At the outset of the war navigational radar was in course of development, but man-made lighting on the ground could still be useful as a navigational and targeting aid for bombing raiders. Well-founded or not, I remember some local feeling that German bomber planes used the bright lights of Dublin, due west of Liverpool, as a navigational aid during their raids on the Merseyside docks. Throughout this country a 'blackout' order existed and was enforced rigorously by civilian ARP (Air Raid Precautions) wardens. Every window in every building had to be 'blacked out' at dusk. Streetlights were either switched off or dimmed and shielded to deflect light downwards. Essential lights such as traffic lights and vehicle headlights were fitted with slotted covers to reduce their beams and deflect them downwards. Lamp posts, telegraph poles and trees on the pavements were painted with white rings to minimise pedestrian accidents in the dark.

Church bells fell silent, as their ringing was to be the sign of an invasion. Decorative iron garden railings were knocked out of their settings and carted away to be melted down as part of a 'scrap' drive to collect materials crucial to the war effort. Air raid shelters were constructed in houses and gardens and streets.

Homes were equipped with stirrup pumps and buckets of water and sand in case of incendiary bombs. Strips of brown paper covered windows to protect against flying glass. A siren sounded when a raid was imminent, a different siren when the danger had passed. The warning siren always evoked some apprehension but less as we grew accustomed to it. The warning siren had an up-and-down pitch and was less piercing than the single high-pitched note of the all clear. Sometimes we slept through the warning siren and were awakened only when all was clear once more. That was a marvellous moment.

During the day barrage balloons tugged against their tethers and drifted over the docks. One afternoon, in broad daylight, an American aeroplane carrying American troops blew up and crashed in a nearby field. We never found out why. The crash shook the house and made all the windows rattle. That was late in the war, in 1944.

That was exceptional. The 'blitz' air raids always took place at night. The first raid on Birkenhead was on 8th/9th August 1940 when a stick of bombs fell across Prenton, without any air raid warning. I remember Mum shrieking 'they are bombing us' and dragging us boys from our beds and rushing us all down to the coat cupboard under the stairs. The nearest bomb fell two or three hundred yards away, killing the maid sleeping in the top floor attic.

This was the first fatality on Merseyside. Thereafter at home we slept on the dining room floor underneath the somewhat doubtful protection of the bed frames brought down stairs.

Bombing raids on Birkenhead continued intermittently until the end of 1941, with air raid warnings sounding on more nights than not. Altogether about four hundred and fifty civilians were killed in Birkenhead by these raids.

During the raids we heard the steady slow drone of heavy planes overhead. Searchlights scanned the sky and the battery of anti-aircraft guns at nearby Holm Lane kept thumping away. I never heard how often they hit their targets but they must have succeeded in forcing the bombers to fly higher and be less accurate with their bomb aiming.

Occasionally the searchlights went out and the guns stopped. They were replaced by the rattle of machine gun fire as fighter planes arrived and engaged the enemy bombers. This was exciting and we cheered. Next morning the ground was littered with pieces of shrapnel.

By and large these unusual happenings were, to us boys, fascinating and stimulating rather than frightening. We were blessed with youthful immortality. Alarm and fear passed over our heads, even when an unexploded bomb had to be removed from the road in front of our house, and even when the front of 13 Osmaston Road itself was blown in by a stray bomb, presumably intended for the docks but jettisoned or badly aimed over our innocuous residential area. This was during the first days of May 1941, known as the 'May Blitz', when Merseyside suffered its 469th air raid. The raids, on eight successive nights, set Liverpool ablaze. From the garden of our home we gazed with awe at the red horizon as the city burned.

These were difficult days even though we boys did not fully appreciate their significance. They were days of retreat, as Britain struggled unsuccessfully to contain the German advance across western Europe. In 1940 The British Expeditionary Force, sent in aid of France when Germany invaded Poland, was cut off and trapped in northern France along with the remains of the French and Belgian armies. In eight days, at the end of May and early June 1940, some 340,000 Allied troops were evacuated from Dunkirk harbour and beaches with the aid of a hastily assembled flotilla of 700 vessels of all sizes: from warships to fishing trawlers, tugboats, lifeboats, pleasure craft, even yachts. More than 200 vessels, including six destroyers, were sunk.

In the following month France fell. German forces were then ranged along the Channel coastline, with the use of all the French airfields and harbours. Britain stood alone when the Battle of Britain was fought in the air in the summer of 1940.

The successful outcome of this battle was the first turning point in the war, Germany's first defeat. Although not publicised at the time the intensive mobilisation on the home front was beginning to make real progress. Farmers increased by one half the acreage of land under cultivation. The output of fighter planes from the factories rose dramatically from 256 in April to 467 in September 1940, and fighter command emerged from the Battle of Britain with more aircraft than it possessed at the start.

This good news was followed, but not for a whole year, by further encouraging events. In June 1941 Hitler abandoned plans to invade England and, instead, invaded Russia. In December 1941 the Japanese attack at Pearl Harbor brought the United States into the war. In July and October 1942 the battles of El Alamein turned the tide on the Egyptian coast.

None of these events directly affected our family, but in 1942 a bombshell of a different kind fell on our household. Dad received his calling up papers. This had not been expected. As the war proceeded the age at which able-bodied men were conscripted into the armed forces was gradually raised up to the age of 41 and Dad, at the age of 40, was just caught. He was enlisted in the Royal Army Service Corps, based at Catterick, Yorkshire, but soon transferred to the Royal Army Pay Corps. The pay corps was responsible for administering soldiers' pay and all other financial matters. He was too old to be commissioned in any other regiment or corps, so in due course he was commissioned as a paymaster.

A worse blow followed when he was posted abroad to India, with all the dangers involved in travelling there by ship. The route through the Mediterranean Sea and the Suez canal was closed. Instead Dad had to sail down the Atlantic coast of west Africa, infested as it was with the ever lurking German submarines, and thence round the Cape and up to his destination at Meerut, north of Delhi. This was not a battle zone, but Meerut was the headquarters of the Indian independence movement. This movement was hostile to the British. So the British troops were confined to their barracks, a debilitating environment, for year after year.

Communication between my parents was limited and uncertain. There was of course no contact by telephone or any of the modern radio links. They wrote to each other every day, numbering their letters so the recipient would know if any had gone astray. Censors opened and read the letters to make sure they contained no information of assistance to the enemy. When letters did arrive they were comforting and reassuring, although already days or weeks out of date.

Like so many other women at the time, in these conditions Mum had to soldier on alone with the care and upbringing of two teenage boys. Life cannot have been much fun for her. Not surprisingly she was lonely, at times depressed.

She could be formidable. Clifford and I were at school during the day. He attended a local secondary school in Birkenhead Park and was quite mischievous. On one autumn day his headmaster Mr Ure summoned Mum to come and see him at the school on a 'serious' matter. When she entered his room he confronted her with a long face. Clifford, he said, had been caught stealing apples in a nearby orchard. Quick as a flash she replied, 'Oh, headmaster, boys will be boys. Boys have been 'scrumping' apples from the time of Adam.' The headmaster said he took a serious view of this in wartime. Not to be outdone Mum then commented, with appropriate emphasis, that Clifford's father had been unable to come because he had been stationed in India for the past two years. After a pause, somewhat chastened, the headmaster muttered he would say no more about this incident.

One end of Osmaston Road adjoined Woodchurch Road, a long road stretching from the village of Woodchurch, up Swan Hill and into Birkenhead. Before the war a large 'Co-op' laundry, with a tall factory chimney, had been built in the open fields near Woodchurch. The laundry vans were horse-drawn and I remember seeing the horses labouring up Swan Hill, tired out by the time they passed the end of Osmaston Road, and even more weary when they returned in the late afternoon after a day's work in the streets of Birkenhead. At home we wondered

13 Osmaston Road, taken in 1993.

why a site had been chosen so far away from where most of the laundry's customers and workers lived.

Until 1943 I attended Woodchurch Road School. This school was housed in a substantial building erected by the local authority and opened in 1905 as an elementary school for boys and girls with separate playgrounds. I was in a class of forty pupils with sandbags against the windows and a bomb crater in the girls' playground where the school shelter had been destroyed by a direct hit in May 1941. Next to the playground was a large empty site, where several houses had also been demolished by bombing.

I recall the teacher, Mrs Harrison, coping magnificently with a large assorted group of pupils. Every morning she chalked the times tables up to twelve on the blackboard and we had to recite these aloud in unison. Whatever may be said for modern teaching methods, this worked well.

On reflection, when I remember the conditions in which everyone lived, it is remarkable that the education of children continued so well at that time.

Woodchurch Road School.

Indeed, continuing to teach young children at all demonstrated an impressive determination to carry on 'business as usual', a sign often seen displayed on damaged shops and offices.

In the classroom the desks were raked, and periodic tests dictated whereabouts each pupil sat. I remember sitting at the back on the top row, which meant I was top of the class. This was not altogether desirable, because on one occasion when Mrs Harrison left the room I was the boy she called upon to sit in front in her elevated desk. On her return I had to tell her which boys had been talking. I was very naïve in those days and told her. This meant that at the end of the afternoon I got thumped in the playground and never again wanted to be top boy.

Each day I came home for lunch. So I walked to and from school twice a day, about a mile or so each way, carrying my gas mask in my satchel. Mum often kept me home as company for her. In my term reports the headmaster repeatedly expressed concern at my frequent absences.

Dad in the army.

The underlying problem was that Mum had no social life. In wartime conditions social life, inevitably, was limited. Two of her sisters lived within walking distance, but for reasons I never understood she did not get on with either of them. The neighbours were a decent lot but, unhappily, friendship with them and others was ruled out, for a different reason. Sadly, the source of this problem was religion.

My father had been brought up by his parents in Birkenhead where my grandfather was a warehouseman. They belonged to the Plymouth Brethren, a strict nonconformist sect. This sect eschewed social contact with non-Brethren. They carried to an inordinate length the Pauline adjuration to the Corinthians to 'be ye not unequally yoked to unbelievers … come out from among them and be separate.' Dad had absorbed and practised this severe and unattractive teaching. Mum was brought up as a member of the Church of England. She married Dad in an Anglican church, but after her marriage she fell into line with him.

The snag was that there were no Plymouth Brethren nearby with whom Mum could establish a friendship. The hall we attended for Sunday services was in the heart of Birkenhead, a district which after the war was regarded as slums. The Plymouth Brethren living there, or the few who attended Camden Hall from Prenton, were 'working-class' folk who were not at ease with Mum, nor she with them.

My father was not able to return home from India until after the end of the war. The war with Germany ended on 8th May 1945, celebrated as VE Day (Victory in Europe Day). Some months later, after atomic bombs had been dropped on Hiroshima and Nagasaki, the war with Japan ended on 15th August with celebrations on VJ Day (Victory in Japan Day). Repatriating thousands of troops from different parts of the world, all anxious to return home as soon as possible, was a complex and protracted exercise. Even with some compassionate priority because of Mum's health my father did not return home until 1946. They had not met or spoken to each other for more than three years. He resumed his work at the bank but, as became apparent, his years abroad had unsettled him.

CHAPTER 3

Birkenhead School
Noctorum: September 1943

AS THE WAR changed life on a larger scale my life also changed at the personal level. One day early in 1943, when I had stayed at home as Mum's comforter, a boy was sent by my school – we had no telephone in the house – to enquire if my mother wished me to sit the scholarship examination for Birkenhead School.

This is a fine school. It was founded in 1860 as an independent school for boys when Birkenhead was growing rapidly. Two historic features are worth a passing mention: first, the origin of the school motto. The school moved to its present premises on Shrewsbury Road on 2nd November 1871. This was within the octave of All Saints' Day, 1st November, and the Gospel reading appointed for that day comprised the beatitudes. The school motto 'Beati mundo corde' (Blessed are the pure in heart) was then chosen from that reading.

The school badge is also of interest. From 1871 onwards, if not before, the arms used by the school included a quartered shield with a lion and a crozier. These were the arms of Birkenhead priory. The borough of Birkenhead adopted them later when it received its charter in 1878.

The school prospered in the 19th century. Later, faced with the economic stringency of the 1930s and a decline in the number of pupils, the school became the recipient of a 'direct grant' from central government. It did so without losing its independence. In return for an annual subvention the school admitted a quarter of its intake from state elementary schools. That was in 1935.

I duly attended an all-day examination at the school with numerous other boys. Despite my dismal attendance record at Woodchurch Road School I somehow contrived to pass the exam and survive an interview. I did so even though, to Mum's amazement, I did not know who lived in the Vatican.

I was awarded a scholarship and joined the junior school in September 1943. Aged ten, I was a year younger than most of the other new boys.

The junior school was accommodated in a large house (Overdale) on the edge of the school grounds but separate from the senior school. An old boy, H Graham White, who was a member of Parliament for Birkenhead, had given this

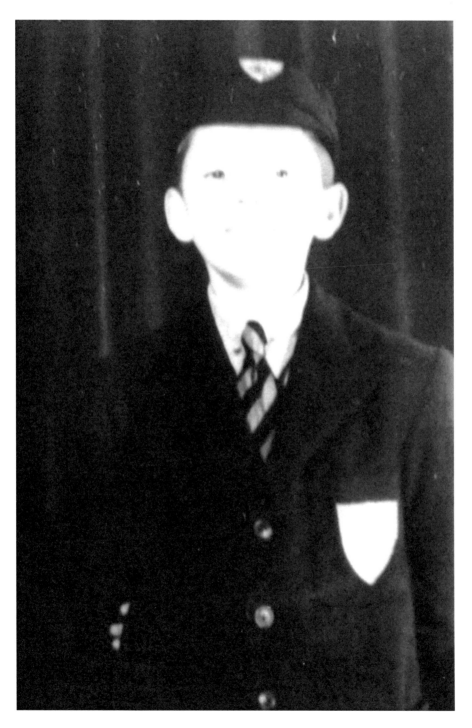

Aged ten.

Birkenhead School campus in 1950s.

to the school in 1931. The form rooms were heated with open coal fires and, as with most scholastic activities at the school, the boys were listed and seated in alphabetical order. So, in winter, Austin and Bennett sat by the fire and were scorched and Williamson sat next to the windows and froze. My desk was more-or-less midway. Our desks were equipped with inkwells, and we used 'dip in' pens and nibs. Blotting paper was an essential accessory but this did not excuse us from presenting our work neatly. Fountain pens were slowly coming into use but they were comparatively expensive.

To me this new school environment was absorbing: different teachers, different companions, new subjects such as French and Latin and botany, and school games. On Saturday mornings the headmaster of the junior school, Rev C A Macvicar, read out in assembly the weekly form orders. He was the school chaplain, known to the boys as 'Chuck Macvicar' because he was prone to throw books at boys when exasperated, although I never saw him do this. His standard punishment for miscreants was to require them to dig out twenty-five daisy weeds, or more, from the school cricket field. He disposed of these in a waste basket in the staff common room. This was well known, and the bolder boys used to creep into this room in the absence of the masters, fish out the daises, and then sell them to other boys. Sometimes the same daisy plants circulated in and out two or three times, but Chuck never seemed to notice that the plants being proffered to him had obviously been dead for a long time.

He was another generous benefactor. He lived in Bidston Road, next door to the 'new schools' block, in a substantial house he bequeathed to the school when he died in 1954.

The school went through a difficult period in the early years of the war. It was in a dangerous area. The governors rejected the possibility of evacuation, partly owing to financial difficulties and partly because the school was two miles or so away from the docks which were the obvious target for air attack. Instead the school cellars were adapted for use as air raid shelters. On the night of 12th/23th March 1941, when Birkenhead suffered its most severe attack and 288 civilians were killed, a shower of incendiary bombs fell on the school campus, one bomb dropping on the junior school building and another on the main hall. Two buildings near the school, St Saviour's church and the adjoining Caernarvon Castle hostelry, were badly hit. The church was severely damaged and the public house totally destroyed. This vacant site was a useful short cut for me when walking to and from school, although the willow-herb spreading over the debris gave the plot a rather depressing, desolate look.

Not surprisingly, pupil numbers dropped and finance became difficult. The younger masters had gone off to the war. The school was kept going by an excellent but ageing headmaster, W F Bushell, and some middle-aged masters, aided by several young mistresses. The art mistress Miss Andrew was totally unable to keep order. Sam Watson, the English master in the adjoining room, used to come and scowl threateningly at us through the glass door of her room. Efficient teaching was to some extent hampered by a shortage of new books and modern equipment. In the junior school woodwork lessons suffered from lack of wood; in the senior school chemistry experiments were limited. These were days of austerity, days of four-page newspapers.

In those years it was quite common for some of the masters in 'public' schools to be clergymen. In the 1940s three masters at Birkenhead School were in Holy

*After the blitz in 1941: St Saviour's church, with remains of
Caernarvon Castle hotel in foreground.*

Orders. Religion loomed much larger in schools then. On Sunday afternoons one of the science masters, W T C Rankin, ran a school branch of the Crusaders' Union, a nationwide interdenominational evangelical youth organisation. I attended these services each Sunday.

I interpose here that, throughout the country at that time, Sundays were very quiet days. They were 'days of rest'. Then, nationwide, there were no organised games or sports and all substantial shops were closed. Buses and trains provided limited services but, in general, the roads and town centres were empty. At my home games, indoor and outdoor, were not permitted, nor was listening to the wireless or reading Sunday newspapers or doing school homework. Reading 'serious' books was acceptable, as was a gentle walk. I remember coping with *Foxe's Book of Martyrs* and attending church, of one form or another, at least once and often twice each Sunday. It is difficult now to envisage this strict form of family and national way of life.

Early Years

As explained by Mr Bushell in his book *School Memories*, Birkenhead School underwent something of a fiscal renaissance in 1944. Following the Education Act of that year, the so-called 'Butler' Act, the school enlarged its annual intake from two forms to three. This became possible because the local authority exercised its right under the Butler Act to pay the fees of a number of Birkenhead boys it selected through its own examination. So from 1945 onwards two entrance examinations were held each year: one by the local authority for Birkenhead boys, and another by the school for boys from anywhere. The local authority paid the school fees for the former; the fees for the latter were based on parental income, on a generous basis, the balance being paid by central government. For a reason I never understood, consequential reorganisation within the school meant that in September 1944 nine boys, of whom I was one, passed directly from form 1B into forms 3A and 3B.

'Skipping' a form in this way was, for me, not without its drawbacks. The age gap between me and most other boys in my new form widened further. I was now two years younger than my fellow pupils. As a small, quiet chap I did not mix easily or make friends with older, bigger and more ebullient boys. In some subjects, particularly mathematics, I never wholly made up for the lost year.

At school we played rugby, hockey and cricket in the three school terms. The head groundsman George Smoker had himself been an outstanding cricketer, playing for Hampshire and against the legendary W G Grace. Although I was not much good at team games I was competent enough to enjoy playing. The school had three fives courts and I liked playing there in the school holidays. Two courts were in the Rugby style, and one in the Eton style with buttress and other hazards. I preferred the simple Rugby style.

Until he retired in 1946 the headmaster Mr Bushell personally maintained and repaired several shabby pairs of fives gloves, with a small supply of balls. Replacements were not readily available. He kept them on a table outside the door of his study, and to borrow them we had to walk through his garden along a path beside his study windows and into his house. He was a kindly man but, even so, as a young boy I was somewhat in awe of him and always slightly apprehensive in case I met him face to face. When I was at the top of the school we were allowed to play squash at the nearby Constitutional Club, which I did several times, presumably with a racket provided by the club.

Boxing was a different matter. An activity whose sole aim is to hit and hurt is not my idea of a game or sport. Each year in January every boy in the senior school boxed three rounds in the boxing ring erected in the school gym. I hated this, although it stood me in good stead at a later stage in my life.

Towards the end of the Lent term all boys engaged in athletics, under the watchful eye of C W Jones. The prelude to the competitive events was that on several days each boy, whatever his ability, sought to attain specified 'standards', varying according to age, in a range of field and track events.

Charlie Jones was a formidable presence in the school. He was a physical training expert and had played rugby for Wales. As we sat cross-legged and barefooted on the floor of the gym he often exhorted us with George Bernard Shaw's aphorism: 'He who can, does; he who cannot, teaches.' Even then I thought this was an extraordinarily tactless observation for him to make inside the school where he worked.

My participation in extracurricular events was limited. I was not a boy scout or, later, a member of the school's officer cadet force. When those weekly sessions took place I felt something of an outcast. My acting career came to an abrupt end when Mum attended a school production and saw me on the school stage dressed and made up as a pretty girl. The school had to manage without me on its visits to a local farm to help lift the potato crop. Mum said that was not what we went to school to do. Cinemas were taboo. In the eyes of the Plymouth Brethren these were Godless places, encouraging immorality irrespective of the content of the particular film. I had to attend upon a mystified headmaster and try to explain why I was not going to Liverpool with the other senior boys to see Laurence Olivier's acclaimed portrayal of Henry V. It was all highly embarrassing.

One extramural activity which did find favour at home was the school's natural history society and field club, run by 'Daddy' Rankin. We were known as the 'bug hunters'. In the school there were talks and film shows. Sometimes we went out on expeditions on Saturday afternoons, to see the wading birds on Hilbre Island at the mouth of the Dee estuary, or to look for what we could find in Delamere forest in the middle of the Cheshire agricultural plain or among the sand dunes at Freshfield on the Lancashire coast. These trips were fun, a welcome diversion, although I was more adept at climbing the trees in the woods than spotting and identifying the quick-moving small birds.

My only other outdoor relaxation was walking down the hill from home and watching Tranmere Rovers playing football at its nearby stadium, Prenton Park. This, unscathed by the war, was situated on Borough Road between, on one side, a hill up to Tranmere and, on the other, a more gentle slope up to Prenton. After half time the large exit doors were thrown open and it was possible to walk through and watch the rest of the match without payment.

I add, in the nature of an obituary, that this club was established in 1884 and a founder member of division three north of the Football League in 1921. Sadly the club dropped out of the Football League in 2015. Its most successful period was in the early 1990s when in three successive seasons it reached the play-offs to the premier league. One of its players, Harold Bell, made a record 459 consecutive appearances from 1946 to 1955. I watched him play many times.

Despite the hiccups I enjoyed my time at Birkenhead School. I enjoyed the attractive setting of the school, the services in the school chapel, and the general stimulation. Unlike today there was no academic pressure at school or at home. I was introduced to orchestral music by a school visit from a section of the Liverpool Philharmonic Orchestra. I still remember some of the music they played. The conductor put his own words to some bars of 'Eine kleine Nachtmusik': 'When Mozart wrote this tune, he must have been so happy.'

At the age of fourteen I obtained a tolerable school certificate, the equivalent of modern GCSEs. At this stage most boys were sixteen and many then left school. I settled more comfortably in the smaller sixth form, with new and better masters returning from the war. I was more at ease than in the lower forms. For the first time I found my feet academically and I remember wishing I were a boarder in the school's boarding house. I loved history and geography but struggled with French and German. I borrowed history books from Birkenhead public library. I had abandoned Latin some years earlier but I was persuaded to resume it on a one-year cram course. This was not a success, and at the end of the year I failed miserably. My sons have never ceased teasing me for failing the equivalent of a GCSE exam in Latin.

I sat the higher school certificate examinations in the summer of 1949. Somehow I contrived to achieve a distinction in modern history and a credit in geography.

So far as my parents were concerned that was the end of my education. I had reached the top of the school and the next step was to get a job. Attending a university did not enter the picture. The headmaster was horrified when I did not return to school at the beginning of the next term. I was disappointed, especially in the light of his final report: 'He would have been a very strong candidate for a state scholarship or an open scholarship at Oxford or Cambridge if he had stayed at school.' Having left the school on this note, after an undistinguished career, in my wildest dreams I would never have thought that one day I would be honoured by being appointed its president.

First Jobs

CHAPTER 4

Introduction To Law
Port Sunlight: September 1949

WHILE I WAS enjoying the sixth form my brother Clifford had already left his school at the age of sixteen after obtaining his school certificate. He had flung himself enthusiastically into farming in the nearby village of Storeton. In taking this course he was much influenced by our father. Dad had made no further progress at the bank and was attracted by the possibility of retiring and taking up farming. He was intrigued by a book, *The Farming Ladder*, in which the author recounted how he had started from nothing and become a successful farmer. The book was my father's bedside reading, together with the *Farmers Weekly* magazine.

I had no particular plans or aspirations. I had no idea what options were open to a boy in my position. In default of any better proposals the lot fell upon Lloyds Bank. Mum thought I should be in no hurry to start. So after a summer break I applied to the bank for a job. My father took it for granted that, with my higher school certificate, the outcome was a foregone conclusion. Not so. The outcome was totally unexpected. The bank's response was that it had already filled all its vacancies for the current year. I have never ceased to be thankful for that turn of events.

I next applied to Lever Brothers at Port Sunlight. The personnel manager Mr Gould was not happy with my application. He did not mince his words. My place, he told me, was at a university. I said my father considered BAs were 'ten a penny'. He was not impressed. I was taken on as a junior clerk and allocated to the registrars' department.

The function of this department was to act as registrars for Unilever Limited, Lever Brothers' parent company. The head office of Unilever was at Blackfriars in London. Lever Brothers undertook on its behalf the administrative tasks of registering transfers of its stock and paying its dividends. These were part of the responsibility of the company's secretary or a registrar acting on his behalf.

The professional body for company secretaries was the Chartered Institute of Secretaries and this body administered professional examinations. In those days correspondence course 'colleges' provided a valuable service for students who, like me, had a full time job. After a while, with the kindly encouragement of one of the

One of the offices at Port Sunlight.

registrars, I embarked on a correspondence course for the intermediate examinations of this institute. I also attended evening lectures in Liverpool. One of the subjects was elementary law of contract.

This was my first acquaintance with law. I was fascinated. I was intrigued by analysing simple everyday transactions in terms of offer, acceptance, consideration, performance, breach. This introduction to the world of legal principles and concepts whetted my appetite for more. The head of the registrars' department was a solicitor and at times I sneaked a look at his All England law reports, although they did not mean much to me. I passed the exam and began to prepare for the final examinations.

Port Sunlight, situated not far from New Ferry and the river, was a model village built at the turn of the century by William Lever, later Lord Leverhulme, to house employees who worked in his soap factory. He adopted the name of Port Sunlight as an advertisement for his Sunlight soap. He built 800 houses as homes for 3,500 people. A different architect designed each block of houses, and each house was unique. In addition the village included an art gallery, churches, a theatre, a primary school, a public house, a war memorial and many other ancillary buildings.

The factories and offices lay at one end of the village. I worked in one of these offices for five days a week, from 8.30am to 5.30pm. At lunchtime I slipped out to eat my sandwiches in a nearby park and began to read some of the classics such as Trollope and Galsworthy. I explored the village, and looked around the Lever Art Gallery when it was wet.

Like most clerical jobs the work demanded exactness but soon became humdrum and boring. I remember sitting on the upper deck of the bus travelling to work on one dark wet morning and thinking I did not wish to spend the rest of my life doing this. My pay was poor, geared as it was to a boy aged sixteen or seventeen, and I passed most of it to Mum. By then I had two baby sisters at home, Marjorie and Joyce, born in 1948 and in 1949.

CHAPTER 5

The Meerut Photograph
National Service: April 1951

SHORTLY AFTER MY eighteenth birthday in January 1951 I received my calling up papers for two years' national service. National service was introduced in 1949 as a form of peacetime conscription for fit young men. Initially the period of service was eighteen months, but in 1950 this was extended to two years in response to the British involvement in the Korean war. I passed my medical examination as A1 and was allocated to the Royal Army Pay Corps as my father had served in that corps in the war. In April I reported to the pay corps training centre at Devizes, in Wiltshire.

The camp was a mile or so north of the town, straddling the old Roman road (now A361) which runs from Devizes to Avebury and bends around the foot of Silbury Hill. This is the tallest prehistoric man-made mound in Europe, similar in size to some of the smaller Egyptian pyramids.

I had no idea what to expect, and what I found was a rude shock. On arrival I was given an army number (22480012) and a pay book. This book contained a form of short will. Seemingly to bring recruits down to earth, the date on this specimen will form was 5th August 1914, all too vividly reminiscent of the horrors of that war. I was issued with khaki battle dress and boots and leggings, and clothed head to foot in army clothing. I cannot recall what happened to my 'civvy' clothes, but I think they must have been posted home. After a day or two I was issued with a rifle.

I slept in a wooden hut with fifteen other new recruits, all as nervous as I was. Every day we had a non-stop programme. We spent the whole of our first weekend 'bulling' our boots with spit and polish (literally), learning how to 'blanco' our belts, and marking our clothing with the last four digits of our army numbers. The boot brushes must have been of a high quality. Sixty years later I still use mine.

We underwent basic training for several weeks: marching, drilling ('square bashing'), physical training, hut inspections, learning how to shoot with a rifle and sten gun and how and when to salute an officer. We wore masks in a gas filled room, bayoneted the guts of an all-too-realistic straw dummy and crawled with a rifle and kit through muddy streams. This was my first experience of living away from home. I was homesick.

National service, 1952.

Recruits were given a weekend's leave every four weeks, and on Friday evenings I travelled home overnight by coach. These monthly trips cost £2, and as pay was poor this left me with very little money to buy buns or tea in the NAAFI canteen. For the first eighteen months national servicemen were paid at an appreciably lower rate than their counterparts in the regular army. I was paid 25*s* (£1.25) a week, of which I sent 10*s* 6*d* home. Once again money was tight.

Basic training was followed by 'technical' training. I was put on an adding machine course because I had some familiarity with these machines in Lever Brothers.

After some weeks three of the recruits in my intake were selected as possible candidates for officer training. I was one. We were sent to a Wiltshire village, Barton Stacey, for a residential interview by a War Office Selection Board (WOSB). The candidates were from a wide spread of regiments and different corps and backgrounds. We were divided into groups of about a dozen. The tests included participating in group discussions, standing up and giving a talk for ten minutes on a self-selected subject, and taking charge in an outdoor exercise calling for initiative and 'lateral thinking'. Some of the candidates were from famous public schools. They had been active in their school cadet forces and were now serving in renowned guards regiments. Delightful as they were, they had a degree of self-confidence I found disconcerting. I was not at ease and I failed. I returned to Devizes to continue my training as a machine operator.

Then, not for the first or last time, I had a remarkable stroke of good fortune. The officer in charge of my company in Devizes was a Major Davies. Next time I returned home I recognised Major Davies' face on one of the group photographs my father had brought home from India. They had served together in Meerut during the war. Dad then wrote to him, and Major Davies sent for me. The upshot was that, very kindly, he decided to let me have a second try at WOSB. But first he sent me to train further under the weapon training officer, Captain Upington. He was a captain in the Royal Ulster Rifles who had lost his right arm in the war. His aim was to make me more self-confident and forceful. I had to boss and shout at recruits when they went to the rifle ranges. This was not altogether easy because I had no rank or authority over them. I too was a newly arrived recruit in course of training.

Following several weeks of this treatment I returned to Barton Stacey to try again. This time I scraped through. I say 'scraped through' advisedly. After the board had announced its decisions the presiding officer, a lieutenant-general, took the unusual step of calling me aside. He said he had confidence in me and it was up to me to show he was right. From this I inferred the outcome had not been clear-cut and that he had saved the day for me.

The next step was to attend the Mons officers' training unit in Aldershot. Mons was renowned for Regimental Sergeant Major Brittain, reputed to have the loudest voice in the British army. Here the atmosphere was very different from Devizes. There were several hundred officer cadets, from many different corps: gunners, sappers, engineers and others. There were only two representatives from the pay corps. All the cadets were enthusiastic and anxious to succeed. We wore a distinctive white disc behind our different beret badges. We all dreaded the prospect of being returned to our units (RTU) as unsuitable.

The basic training lasted for some weeks. The going could be quite tough, but the officers in charge were always encouraging and the sergeants treated us like gentlemen. Two recollections will suffice. Our only sport was boxing. Having boxed at school I knew what to expect. I knew I had to be aggressive. I had grown some inches in height since school days but I was as skinny as ever. So I had a good reach but boxed at a very light weight, flyweight (eight stone). Ironically I contrived to win and was awarded a medal. Ironically, because this is the only sports medal I have ever won and it is in the only sport I have ever hated.

The final outdoor exercise involved spending two days on Salisbury Plain. The cadets were divided into two groups. One group had to simulate a dawn attack on the other. We enjoyed throwing thunder flashes and firing flares and blank cartridges. For me the only flaw was that, for the sake of comfort, I foolishly removed my boots when we tried to sleep. That night there was a sharp frost, so next morning getting into my boots and wearing them was somewhat uncomfortable.

I did not greatly mind. I had passed the course, with an above average grade. I mention this only because I remember wishing I had been able to tell my supportive general that, at any rate to some extent, I had vindicated his WOSB decision.

That was the end of the basic training course. The cadets then went their several ways, for further training in their specialities. Two of us returned to Devizes for a further six weeks' training in the work of a paymaster. After Mons this was singularly dull and flat. There was seemingly interminable exposition of the minutiae of running a paymaster's office. The only event I can remember was hearing the announcement of the death of King George VI on the afternoon of 6th February 1952, another occasion imprinted on my mind.

As this course neared its end I was offered the choice of two postings: either go to a pay office in Germany or stay in Devizes as a training officer. I chose the latter. The novelty of living in Germany was attractive, but a sedentary clerical life did not appeal to me. I had seen enough of that in Port Sunlight.

I was commissioned on 7th March 1952 and became a second lieutenant. I owed this to my father, for it was his intervention with Major Davies which had given me a second chance. I bought (second hand) my officer's dress uniform and polished leather 'Sam Browne' belt. After a short leave I took up my duties as the officer in charge of two platoons of new recruits. My fame must have gone before me because I was invited to join the unit's boxing team. I declined.

It was a strange transition. Less than a year previously I had been a raw recruit myself. Now the recruits were saluting me and addressing me as 'sir'. I was only nineteen years old.

Life in the officers' mess was comfortable. It was a civilised place, a short walk from the camp, with the companionship of a dozen or so national service subalterns as well as more senior officers. I had a batman to polish my boots and make my bed. For the first time in my life I did not have to count every penny, and I was able to save some money from my officers' pay.

The only unwelcome duty was taking a turn at being the orderly officer. The orderly officer was an officer who was on duty all night or all weekend. One of his duties was to get up in the middle of the night and go to the camp and order the sentry to call out the guard, to make sure they were awake and alert. Next morning the orderly officer had to make an oral report to the adjutant. Normally there was 'nothing to report'. One night when I was orderly officer there was a fire. Next morning I presented myself to the adjutant and said, 'Nothing to report except the fire.' 'Isn't that enough for one night?' was his sarcastic response.

In these early years after the war church attendance was much more general than it is today. Two of my fellow subalterns were destined to become clergymen, and the nearby church on the edge of Devizes was packed on Sunday mornings. I decided to become a member of the Church of England.

Along with two other national service officers I was baptised and confirmed early in 1953. The baptismal part of the service was conducted by candlelight because the electricity had failed. By coincidental symbolism, as we moved forward from the font towards the altar for the second part of the service the darkness and shadows were dramatically dispelled and the church was bathed in brilliant light as the electricity was restored.

I made some good friends: Denis High, Mark Hughes and Alan Speed. Shortly before Denis completed his two years in October 1952 we had a jolly weekend jaunt in the west country, driven by Denis in his father's car. It was a memorable trip. After leaving the army Denis was ordained as a priest in the Church of England, with a London parish. He died very young. Mark went on to Balliol College, Oxford. He was a man of parts. He had a good voice and was mad on Gilbert and Sullivan. He played rugby for Durham and became the Member of Parliament for Durham. He also died young. *Sic transit gloria mundi.* To my regret I lost touch with Alan.

In the meantime my parents had changed their views about university education. Mum in particular became reconciled to the idea that after my spell of national service my next step should be to go to a university to study law since I was so attracted by this subject. The cheapest means to this end was that I should attend Liverpool University but live at home. I would be eligible for a subsistence grant from Cheshire county council.

Naturally I was delighted at this change of direction. I got in touch with the law faculty at Liverpool University, and the dean offered me a place for September 1953. I made good my deficiency in Latin with the aid of yet another correspondence course while I was still in Devizes.

When the commandant, Colonel Malpass, heard I was starting at Liverpool University in the autumn he kindly offered to arrange with the war office to extend my service until then. Financially this was highly attractive but I had to decline as I had already arranged to resume work at Port Sunlight. I left the army in April 1953 and returned to Lever Brothers for the intervening six months.

Universities

CHAPTER 6

Learning The Law
Heswall and Liverpool: 1953

IN THE SUMMER of 1953, shortly after the Coronation of Queen Elizabeth II and news that a British expedition had conquered Everest, my parents moved house from Prenton to Heswall on the far side of Wirral. This was a small town on a red sandstone ridge overlooking the wide river Dee estuary. It was the highest point in Wirral. The local saying, not altogether fair, was that if you could see across to the Halkyn hills in north Wales it was about to rain, and if you could not it was already raining.

The move was precipitated by the need for more bedroom accommodation. The three bedrooms plus box room in the house in Osmaston Road were no longer adequate for four adults and the two girls. The house in Heswall was bigger. It was a tall house approached up a short steep driveway and comprised three floors and, at the front of the house, a large semi-basement cellar. There were three bedrooms on the first floor and two on the second floor. Clifford and I used these two rooms on the top floor. My bedroom had a dormer window below which a long coil of rope was fastened to the floor as a means of escape in case of fire. Happily I never had to use this emergency exit. It was a long drop to the ground and I was never much good at climbing up and down the ropes in the school gym.

The move to Heswall had an unfortunate consequence. My father had one sibling, a younger sister named Margaret Irene but known to everyone as Daisy. She had a large family, ultimately nine children. She and her husband Alfred and family and her parents, that is, my grandparents, lived in Oxton, a village on the outskirts of Birkenhead. Alfred ran a business as a cobbler in a cornershop, with living accommodation behind the shop and upstairs. As my father did not always see eye-to-eye with his sister we had very little contact with her and her family, and after we left Prenton we lost touch completely.

September 1953 saw the start of my university career. The main buildings of Liverpool University were at the top of Brownlow Hill, five minutes' walk from the city centre. Mercifully, unlike the blocks of houses at the foot of the hill, these buildings had emerged largely unscathed from the wartime blitz.

House in Heswall.

Cheek by jowl with the main university buildings, and resembling a huge blitzed site, was an extensive boarded-off area enclosing the foundations and crypt of the unfinished Roman Catholic cathedral. The origin of this project, indirectly, was the Irish potato famine in the mid-19th century. Half a million Irish, mostly Roman Catholic, fled to England. Some went on to North America but many stayed in Liverpool. The increase in the Roman Catholic population in the city prompted a decision, in the late 1850s, to build a cathedral. After an abortive start in Everton, a nine-acre site was bought at the top of Brownlow Hill. In 1930 Sir Edwin Lutyens was commissioned to provide a design which would be an appropriate response to the Neo-Gothic Anglican cathedral, designed by Giles Gilbert Scott, then being built further along Hope Street. Lutyens' design was intended to create a massive structure which would have been the second largest church in the world with the world's largest dome. Building work began in 1933, but did not proceed beyond the foundations and crypt before the outbreak of war forced construction to stop. The building works had not proceeded further when I was a student at the university in the 1950s. Later, a less ambitious but striking building was completed in 1967.

The university's faculty of law was located at one corner of Abercromby Square, a short walk from the main buildings. This was a handsome square, named after General Sir Ralph Abercromby, commander of the British army in Egypt, who was killed at the battle of Alexandria in 1801. Terraced houses, built mainly in the 1820s, were set round the four sides of a central garden.

This faculty comprised about ninety students, with one third admitted each year for a three-year course. Nearly all had come straight from school, and most were articled to solicitors practising in Liverpool. They spent most of their time in their offices and came to the faculty building only for the lectures. Like me, nearly all of them lived at home. We had half a dozen lectures each week, and the law faculty's Legal Society met on Friday afternoons. Then the faculty building came alive, for at other times it was almost wholly deserted.

We did not see much of our lecturers. With only two exceptions they were busy practising barristers. As soon as they had delivered their lectures they, like the students, slipped away from Abercromby Square and hastened back to their other work.

As is to be expected, the quality of the lectures varied: some were excellent, others not so good. A disappointing feature of the teaching was that the lectures were not supplemented by any form of supervisions or tutorials. This may have been commonplace in other 'red brick' universities in those days. Dr Farran and Professor Turner were exceptions. In particular Joe Turner held tutorials in his home in Sefton Park on Sunday mornings. These were invaluable.

I travelled into the university each weekday. I did so irrespective of whether I had any lectures fixed for that day. Mum took the view that attending a university was rather like going to school. I should go there every day, and be there all day. I was not expected to stay at home. So I left the house at about 8.30am, with my father giving me a lift so far as Birkenhead, and I returned at about 6pm.

I arrived at the university about 9.30am. My practice was to go to the students' union and read a newspaper. At that early hour there was never any competition for a comfortable seat or a newspaper.

Unless there was a lecture I then spent some hours in the Cohen library, getting to grips with the law. The era of better legal textbooks had barely started. At times it was hard going, but always interesting and satisfying. I ate my sandwiches in a former chapel. Sometimes I had a game of squash with one of my friends. The law students were noticeable by their absence.

As to money, I passed the whole of my subsistence allowance to Mum. I met all my expenses, for travelling and textbooks and so on, out of the money I had saved in the army.

Each vacation I had a different job: a nurse in a mental hospital at Chester, a porter at Woodside railway station, a guinea-pig at the common cold research unit on Salisbury Plain, a gillie on Loch Awe in Scotland.

The jobs in the summer vacation were more fun. I was keen to travel and in my first long vacation I had a job in a department store in Oslo, which gave me an opportunity to see something of Norway. To enable me to afford the train fare to visit Stockholm and have a glimpse of Sweden I limited myself to one hot meal each third day.

Every summer I spent some weeks as the 'organiser', responsible for everything except cooking, at a fruit-picking farm near Wisbech. This was arranged by the National Union of Students, principally for students from the continent. It gave me some insight into the differing work appetites of the several nationalities.

Towards the end of the summer vacation I always undertook a fortnight's training in the army emergency reserve at a camp near Kidderminster, the closest to Wirral. This was the most financially profitable of all my jobs. I was promoted to 'lieutenant and paymaster' in 1956.

In 1956 a travel scholarship enabled me to attend a summer school on international law at The Hague. This was interesting and I stayed a couple of weeks but, like most young people, I was anxious to visit other places. So I cut short my time in The Hague and returned home by a circuitous route: Amsterdam, Cologne, up the Rhine to Bonn and Koblenz and then the Moselle to Cochem. I lingered there for a day or two while the Weinfest was held, and completed my journey back to the Wisbech farm via Luxembourg, Rheims and Paris. I have to say, although this may seem ungrateful, that I learned more from my travelling than I did in The Hague.

Whilst at Liverpool I had to decide what I should do after I had obtained my degree. Qualifying as a solicitor was out of the question, on financial grounds. In those days being articled to a solicitor was expensive. In Liverpool the premium was about £500 and in Birkenhead £250. So I turned my attention to the Bar.

Here also, being admitted to one of the four Inns of Court cost money. Happily, the Inns offered scholarships. At that time Middle Temple was the only Inn offering an entrance scholarship without examination. I jumped at this opportunity. In April

1955 I was awarded a Blackstone entrance scholarship and the following month became a student member of the Inn.

I then began 'eating my dinners' in the magnificent and historic Middle Temple hall. This hall, built in 1570, is spanned by a fine double hammer beam roof carved by the carpenter of Queen Elizabeth I from the oak of Windsor Forest. It was the venue of the first performance of *Twelfth Night* in 1602. The hall has remained virtually unaltered, save that the elaborately carved wooden screen was extensively damaged in the war, since repaired with great skill. The long bench table, made in one piece of three 29-feet oak planks floated down the river from Windsor, was installed before the hall was completed. Sir Francis Drake dined at this table on 4th August 1580 on his return from a marauding raid on the Spanish Main.

Memory of the Elizabethan maritime era has been perpetuated in the Inn. According to longstanding oral tradition, when Drake's ship *The Golden Hind* was in the breaker's yard at Deptford some years later the Inn managed to retrieve the ship's main hatch cover. This was made into a table, known as 'the cupboard', which is the centrepiece of formal activities in the Inn. The register of calls is placed upon it when members are called to the Bar.

In the 1950s Bar students were required to keep twelve terms by attending their Inns and eating six dinners each term, or three dinners each term if they were university students. I travelled from Merseyside to London for this purpose. What then happened on one of my visits from Liverpool was, beyond question, the most fortunate happening of my many strokes of good fortune.

In those days the Bar was at a low ebb. There was an acute shortage of work for barristers, and most budding lawyers chose to become solicitors. In the Inns most of the students were from overseas, principally Africa. So white faces stood out a mile, the more so if the student was a young woman. It was while attending the Inn to eat one of my dinners in 1956 that I happened to spot Jennifer Thomas, an undergraduate reading law at Girton College, Cambridge. It was some time before our paths crossed again.

In my third year at Liverpool I spent a day in a solicitor's office. Late in the afternoon a client came into the office to make her will. She explained the long-term dispositions she wished to make. The solicitor advised her that these were not possible. Eventually she said, in a hushed and hesitant voice, that she believed in reincarnation. What she really wanted to do, she said, was to leave her money in terms enabling her to reclaim it when she was reincarnated.

It was an eerie moment as solicitor and client sat in silence looking at each other while the light faded both outside and inside the office. The solicitor was lost for words. His client had nothing else to say, and after a while she left the building. I never heard the outcome.

My greatest friend was one of the few law students at Liverpool not intending to practise as a solicitor: Brandon Jackson. His calling was the church. He was president of his hall of residence and always full of fun and enthusiasm. He went on to Oxford University and was ordained. Over the years our friendship has always continued even though we have lived in different parts of the country.

My time at Liverpool University was running out. Dr Farran took a kindly interest in me and suggested I would have more opportunities if, after Liverpool, I went to Oxford for a post-graduate degree there. He introduced me to one of the colleges. Much later, after the degree results were announced and I had obtained a first, the dean of the faculty Professor Seaborne Davies asked me about my future plans. I mentioned Dr Farran's suggestion. His counter proposal was that I would be better suited to Trinity Hall, Cambridge, one of the smaller colleges and renowned for its law.

I took his advice and went to Trinity Hall in July 1956 for an interview. There I met Trevor Thomas, one of the law dons, and the dean Robert Runcie. Both were delightful men and exceptionally able. Trevor Thomas subsequently became the vice-chancellor of Liverpool University. Robert Runcie had a distinguished career in the Church of England and ultimately became archbishop of Canterbury.

The outcome of my visit was that the college offered me a place for the forthcoming term. I was awarded a state scholarship, which would be sufficient for my living expenses at Cambridge. The college asked me for £35 caution money in advance. By now my army pay savings had run out. Embarrassingly I had to keep the college waiting for some weeks until I had acquired enough from my farm camp earnings

Meanwhile Clifford had left home. In January 1955, with my aid as his best man, he had married Joan Ireland. They had met while working on a farm in Storeton, Wirral. After they married they bought a farm in Anglesey, in an idyllic setting with a view across to Snowdonia and stone walls around the fields. The house was approached up a wooded drive lined with daffodils, past a lodge at the gate. They worked hard and built up a fine herd of pedigree Jersey cows, which added to the scenery. Here they brought up their five children, three daughters and then two sons. Joan's gift for music has passed down to her children and grandchildren.

CHAPTER 7

Learning More Law
Cambridge: October 1956

WHEN I WENT up to Cambridge my intention was to take the course for the postgraduate LLB degree in the first of my two years and undertake some research in the second year. When I arrived the plan changed. Mr Thomas and his colleague Dr T Ellis Lewis decided I would benefit more from my time in Cambridge if in my first year I took part II of the law tripos and in the second year the LLB course. Supervisions in groups of three or four undergraduates and weekly essay writing were a central feature of teaching law in Cambridge. These were part of the tripos course but not of the LLB course. It would be unfortunate, they said, if I were to miss this opportunity while I was at Cambridge. They were absolutely right. It was through these supervisions that I learned to think.

Cambridge had many advantages over Liverpool. The Backs are a beautiful stretch of the river Cam and Trinity Hall abuts directly onto them. The undergraduates were more mature. They had already completed their national service, and some had fought in Korea. They lived in college, as did the master and some of the dons, or in 'digs' nearby. So little or no time was wasted travelling to and fro. The law undergraduates were particularly fortunate because in those days the law faculty and the Squire law library were based in the Old School buildings, a stone's throw from Trinity Hall ('the Hall').

The college was always a lively and friendly place. Even the undergraduates living outside the college had lunch and dinner in the college hall with everyone else. The college chapel held daily services which were well attended, as were the many churches in Cambridge on Sundays.

Religion played quite a large part in the lives of most undergraduates. The incumbent at Great St Mary's, the university church, was Mervyn Stockwood, who later became the bishop of Southwark. He was a gifted and inspiring preacher, and on Sunday evenings the undergraduates queued to get into his church. I often joined the queue.

This high degree of interest in religion must have been a recent development. A year or so later at a dinner for Hall graduates the master Sir Ivor Jennings, a

Working hard: Squire law library, Cambridge.

constitutional lawyer, said that those who had been at the Hall before the war would be surprised at this feature.

My supervisors were the three law dons of the Hall. The third law don was Cecil Turner, a criminal lawyer. Their supervisions were always excellent: interesting, helpful, challenging. As at Liverpool, the quality of the lectures varied. Some were brilliant, most were good, one or two were poor. One lecturer was so indifferent that Mr Turner advised us not to waste our time by attending his lectures.

The daily pattern was that we attended one or two lectures from 9am, followed by a supervision later in the morning or early in the evening. There was no formal tuition in the afternoon, from 2pm to 5pm. These hours were sacrosanct, set aside for games or other relaxation. How different from today. I played squash on the college squash ladder, with indifferent success, reaching only the dizzy height of the college second team. But I enjoyed it.

Another difference was that in those days comparatively few visitors came to Cambridge and all the colleges were open for anyone to walk in and out and through. The large gate in Latham Court in Trinity Hall was kept wide open, as was the facing door into Trinity College. I often walked around the beautiful Trinity backs with their displays of crocus and, later, tulips and cherry blossom. The daffodils usually flowered, unseen, during the Easter vacation. Walks to Grantchester or across the fields to Coton for tea were popular: the M11 motorway did not exist.

My closest friend was Peter Bentley, another lawyer. He was in his final year at the Hall. We spent many afternoons together, mostly walking and talking about everything under the sun. He was awarded a half-blue as a middle distance runner.

In those days all the colleges were single sex and all were 'men only' save for Girton, Newnham and New Hall. Women lawyers were rare birds. In my first year, which coincided with the third year for other undergraduates, there were only half a dozen of them. Four of them were Girton girls. At that time Girton had no law dons of its own, and the supervisions for its handful of lawyers were arranged by the Hall. So we saw these Girton girls in the Hall from time to time. On one occasion I went to a sherry party given by Anthony Bailey in his rooms in college and, behold, I met Jennifer Thomas again.

Thereafter from time to time I travelled to London by train with her and others to eat a dinner in one of the Inns of Court. Like me Jenny came from Cheshire, but she lived at the other end of the county, in Stalybridge, where both her parents were practising doctors.

One morning I took my courage in both hands and invited her to come to the theatre and see John Osborne's new play *Look Back in Anger*. Jenny tells me I went bright red when I invited her on the steps of the Senate House. Also, that during the interval I was so shocked by the language I asked her if she would like to leave. She declined.

At the end of my first year nearly all the Hall lawyers who had completed their third year went down and joined firms of solicitors. The lawyers with whom I had most mixed remained in touch. Some years later ten of us established a practice of meeting for dinner or lunch once a year with our wives. We have continued this practice ever since, save only that our numbers have started to fall as the gods take away, one by one, those whom they love.

As we went our separate ways in June 1957 I undertook my customary fortnight's army training followed, for the last time, by several weeks at a farm camp in Wisbech. Peter Bentley and I then went for a walking holiday on the west coast of Scotland. I retain poignant memories of sharing a double bed in the only 'hotel' on Iona, being drenched on the Isle of Skye, and attending a village concert in Broadford where, two songs apart, the entire programme was in Gaelic. Since then Peter has told many of his friends this was the last time he slept with another man.

Peter obtained a first class degree, and his next step was to head to London and join Linklaters and Paines, the well-known firm of city solicitors. Linklaters was then a much smaller firm because in those days partnerships were limited to twenty partners. I returned to Cambridge for my second year, this time without the aid of supervisions.

In my second year I had a room in college. It was a small room on the second floor of the master's house, overlooking the fellows' garden. I had expected that in the absence of supervisions I would have more time on my hands.

This was not how matters turned out. At the beginning of the year I was invited to supervise two of the Girton lawyers, Rosalyn Cohen and Jean Cardell, for part II of the law tripos. No doubt this was something of a compliment to me but I did wonder how the girls must have felt being landed with a supervisor who had no experience of teaching and was himself still an undergraduate.

Of course teaching is an excellent way of learning, and I found the exercise interesting and stimulating. Happily both girls did well, Ros Cohen obtaining a first. She was destined for a great future in her chosen subject, international law, and became president of the International Court of Justice at The Hague.

Compared with the law tripos few students took the course for the LLB degree, later rechristened the LLM degree. We all fitted into one small lecture room. The atmosphere was quiet and subdued. There was something of a feeling that we had been left behind. My friend Anthony Bailey and I were the only LLB candidates from Trinity Hall.

Meanwhile Jenny had gone to London and was attending lectures at the tutorial firm Gibson and Weldon in Chancery Lane in preparation for her Bar final examinations. She came to Cambridge on a couple of occasions. On one winter's day we had planned to go to a point-to-point race meeting at Cottenham. This was cancelled by a fall of snow. I remember walking along King's Parade with snowflakes on our faces. She came again in the summer after my exams had finished. I had arranged a drinks party in my room but this had to be taken over by my friend Peter Penny as I went to bed feeling unwell.

Peter Penny, a South African lawyer, became a good friend of mine. Years later, after he had returned to Cape Town and married and had a family, Jenny and I were guardians to several of his children when they came to England to complete their school education at Eton or Haileybury. Tragically his elder boy Nicholas, a delightful young man, died very young when he lost his way walking in the snow in a wild part of the Cape.

Toward the end of my second year I had a narrow squeak on the night before the LLB examinations. After supper I was having coffee in someone's room in college. One of the undergraduates was idly playing with an up-ended walking stick, treating it as a golf putter. Then, without warning, his putter turned into a driver and struck me a hefty thwack just above my left eye, creating a bloody mess. Off I went to Addenbrooke's Hospital, but no harm had been done. Next morning I had a huge bruise. One of the Hall law dons, who saw me on my way into the exam room, nearly had a fit. No, I had not walked into a door or fallen off my bicycle. He looked incredulous when I explained what had happened. Needless to say, I did not disclose the identity of the would-be golfer.

Later, having obtained a starred first in both years, I was offered a law fellowship at the Hall. I had greatly enjoyed and benefited from my two years in Cambridge, a high-powered and beautiful place, and this was an attractive proposal. But I did not think this was my metier and I declined. Instead I set myself the daunting task of building up a practice at the Bar in London after taking the Bar examinations.

CHAPTER 8

Bar Finals – The Last Exams
Cornwall: Spring 1958

IN THE SPRING of 1958, during my second year at Cambridge, my parents moved from Heswall to Cornwall. My father had taken the plunge and left the bank and decided to try his hand at farming. They bought an attractive stone cottage at Lanteglos-by-Camelford, north Cornwall, together with a few acres of land. Their cottage rejoiced in the grand name Castle Goff. Some years later Sir John Betjeman, who loved this part of Cornwall, sought to buy it from them.

With Mum, Dad and the girls in Cornwall.

Marjorie and Joyce, now aged ten and eight, attended school in Camelford. The hamlet of Lanteglos, for it was too small to be described as a village, was in a valley graced by a charming grade I listed church dedicated to St Julitta, an early martyr. The church was a classic Cornish parish church, dating back to Norman times.

After leaving Cambridge I went, for the last time, for two weeks' army emergency training. I chose to go to Canterbury where I had never been. At the weekend I came up to London and had lunch with Jenny at St Ermin's hotel, Westminster. Afterwards we walked across Hyde Park to Upper Berkeley Street where Jenny was living. By now she had taken and passed her Bar finals and been called to the Bar. She gave me her lecture notes from Gibson and Weldon.

Equipped with these I travelled home to Cornwall and spent the mornings of the next couple of months digging the garden and every afternoon preparing for my Bar examinations, two very different kinds of hard labour. In September I returned to London and stayed for some nights at the YMCA while I sat the exams. I remember an enormous feeling of relief that I would never have to sit any more examinations for the rest of my life.

Jenny's lecture notes must have been very good because with their aid I passed in class 1 ('certificate of honour'). In November 1958 I was called to the Bar, that is, became entitled to practice as a barrister or, in the old-fashioned nomenclature, as a barrister-at-law. The next step was a pupillage.

At The Bar

CHAPTER 9

Wearing A Wig
Starting at the Bar: November 1958

LIKE MANY BAR students I had no financial resources of my own and now my several exam results helped immensely. Armed with these results I was fortunate to be awarded scholarships by Trinity Hall and Middle Temple totalling £600 for three years.

During my pupillage year I augmented this scholarship income by teaching (supervising) law undergraduates at Cambridge. I spent Friday mornings in chambers in London and, after a cheap lunch with Peter Bentley in a pub at the foot of Fleet Street, I caught a train to Cambridge in time for two hours' supervision of four or five begowned undergraduates in the early evening in a room in Queens' College, followed by the same again on Saturday mornings. On Friday evenings I dined at high table in Queens' and met many interesting people. The master was Arthur Armitage, later Sir Arthur Armitage and vice-chancellor and professor of common law at Manchester University. He was delightful company and ranked among the legal giants of those days. I slept in the college in one of the rooms of Geoffrey Wilson, a law don, overlooking the river Cam and the so-called 'mathematical' wooden bridge.

In the early days, far from being burdensome, these trips were quite exhilarating as well as financially profitable. It was a different matter when I started getting some work of my own. At the beginning of the next academic year, acting on medical advice, I had to abandon further Cambridge supervisions.

Before I left Trinity Hall I gave much thought to my future as a barrister. I never envisaged myself as a cut-and-thrust court advocate in the mould of famous performers such as Marshall Hall and Hartley Shawcross. Something quieter, I thought, would suit me better and the tax Bar, where most of the work is advisory, might be best. Trevor Thomas introduced me to a tax barrister, whose name I regret I cannot now recall. He invited me to lunch in London. He told me he had just left the Bar and advised me against starting at the tax Bar. He had left the Bar because he had fallen out with the head of his chambers and found himself with no practice of his own to carry with him to another set of chambers. Financially he could not afford to start again from the beginning. The reason why, after some years, he had no practice of his own was that most of his work had been 'devilling'. 'Devilling' is, or was, the practice whereby an overworked barrister is assisted by an underemployed barrister who reads his papers and drafts opinions for him to sign. This brings in some money for the 'devil', but the snag is that the devil has no direct contact with the instructing solicitor and, thus, is unable to build up any reputation of his own.

I accepted this advice. This was another stroke of good fortune in my career. Looking back I do not think I would have been as happy with an exclusive diet of tax law as I was with the more varied viands which later came my way.

I then turned my attention to the chancery Bar. My long-suffering mentor, Trevor Thomas, next introduced me to Peter Oliver, a successful barrister who later became Lord Oliver of Aylmerton. He practised at the chancery bar in Lincoln's Inn, at 13 Old Square. He was himself a graduate from Trinity Hall. Indeed at that time several of the barristers in that set of chambers were Hall men. I started with Peter in October 1958, first as his pupil for one year and then as a tenant (member) of the chambers. Little did I foresee I would spend the next happy twenty-five years there.

I was fortunate indeed to join these excellent chambers. The members were an able and successful and congenial group. In the years to come, in addition to Peter Oliver going to the House of Lords, Brian Dillon, Colin Rimer and Richard McCombe went to the Court of Appeal, Bill Blackburne and Bill Charles to the High Court bench and Hazel Williamson became a circuit judge. Tim Pratt, with me at Trinity Hall, was another pupil in chambers. He then then took up residence in the Treasury Solicitor's office and became deputy treasury solicitor and counsel to the speaker of the House of Commons (European legislation), picking up a CB on the way. He and Clifford were godfathers to my eldest child.

When I joined them these chambers had nine members: two silks, of whom one had little work, five established juniors and two barely started juniors. This was typical of chancery chambers in the 1950s. Some were larger, but many sets comprised just three or four members with no silks. Today 13 Old Square, as a result of growth and mergers and now known as Maitland Chambers, is the largest set in Lincoln's Inn with about seventy members of whom twenty-eight are silks.

The impression I have is that this substantial increase in size is partly dictated by economic considerations in the present day management of barristers' chambers and partly a reflection of the overall growth of the Bar, barely 1,900 practising barristers nationwide in the late 1950s and now several times that number.

For one year I lived in a rented room in Tufnell Park, north London, not a very exciting place. My landlady had a cat whose basket was in the room above mine. Many were the nights I was kept awake by this wretched cat scrabbling on the linoleum overhead.

Jenny lived a couple of miles away in Belsize Park, a more salubrious district in northwest London. She shared a pleasant terraced house with three other girls. After being called to the Bar she had a year's pupillage with Gordon Friend, a delightful common lawyer with a general practice. His room was in Paper Buildings in the Temple and overlooked the gardens of the Inner Temple. Fortunately she did not follow one piece of his advice which was 'never marry a man with a first class degree – they never get over it.' She was sure there were exceptions to this rule.

Then she became the personal assistant to Hedley Parker, the legal adviser to the Gas Council. Its offices were at Hyde Park corner. At that time natural gas was being converted into a liquefied form for ease of transport. Liquefied gas occupies 1/600th of the volume of natural gas in its gaseous state. Early in 1959 the world's first ocean cargo of liquefied gas sailed to Britain in the huge *Methane Pioneer*. From there the next step forward in the gas industry was to consider the feasibility of extracting natural gas from under the North Sea. One of Jenny's most interesting tasks at the Gas Council was to investigate the ownership of this seabed. Her report was passed to the chairman. This was the beginning of the exploration for natural gas in the North Sea.

Starting at the Bar involves starting from nothing. The young barrister has to make himself available to pick up any small work coming into chambers which the established barristers are too busy to accept. In chancery chambers the work is entirely civil. There is no criminal work. Typically, in those days County Court work comprised disputes between neighbours or between landlords and tenants. In the High Court young barristers would be instructed to appear on Monday mornings before a chancery judge hearing petitions for orders to wind up companies for non-payment of their debts.

From time to time another source of court work in the chancery division was the court's jurisdiction to supervise the upbringing of children ('minors') by making them wards of court. Young barristers were briefed to appear in disputes between parents about custody of their children or, more controversially, on applications by parents for an order forbidding an allegedly undesirable young man from meeting their daughter, often a girl in her late teens. In those days the age of majority was twenty-one years.

Advisory work occupied most of the time of young chancery barristers. A fruitful source of income was conveyancing (transfer of land). At that time the title to much land was still unregistered. So when ownership changed hands the seller had to produce documents showing a good title for the last thirty years, rather than simply producing a copy of an entry on the land register. This meant that, in the 1960s, title often had to be deduced from a pre-1926 deed, that is, from a deed pre-dating the simplification of land law introduced by the 1925 legislation. Solicitors were often happy to leave these pre-1926 complexities to young counsel.

I received my first set of instructions on the very first day after I was called to the Bar. That was possible in those days. A newly qualified barrister could even appear in court before completing any period of pupillage. Not surprisingly, when I had read my instructions I did not have the faintest idea what to advise. Peter Oliver kindly drafted an opinion for me to sign. The solicitor was so impressed he returned to me again and again.

In those days conferences with barristers were invariably held in barristers' own rooms. The solicitor client and the lay client had to attend upon the barrister. (Even then there were exceptions to every rule. Much later I was instructed to advise the Bank of England in conference. There was no question of the governor coming to my room in Lincoln's Inn. It was taken for granted that I would go to the bank and see him in his majestic surroundings.)

In my second year I had a strange conference. Raggett, the senior clerk at 13 Old Square, offered me a brief to appear in the Court of Appeal. This, he said, will give you a chance to cut your teeth in an appellate court. In those days senior clerks were known by their surnames.

The brief concerned a dispute over a restrictive covenant. I read the papers and had no doubt the client's case was hopeless. It was not surprising she had lost in the High Court. Nor was it surprising her counsel found himself 'unavailable' for a hearing in the Court of Appeal.

A conference was arranged, and the solicitor and his client accompanied by her son duly presented themselves in my room. As gently as I could I spelled out the reasons why I considered the appeal was bound to fail. Whereupon the client whispered in the solicitor's ear and they both left the room, without any explanation, followed shortly by the son. I sat there alone, bemused.

After a while the solicitor returned. He told me his client was in contact with the 'spirits'. On the way over in the car the spirits had advised her to conduct the case herself, but she had decided she would meet me before making her decision. Having met me she had no doubt the spirits were right.

She then conducted her case in person. She lost, but I must add that Lord Denning dissented in her favour.

Lincoln's Inn was an agreeable place to work, with its attractive buildings and spacious gardens. I recall one particular occasion. All courts have robing rooms. Despite this, the practice in Lincoln's Inn was that junior barristers changed in their own rooms and then walked in their robes through Lincoln's Inn and across Carey Street to the back entrance to the Royal Courts of Justice.

Not surprisingly, visitors to the Inn were intrigued by this unusual spectacle and rushed forward to take photographs. One day, after I had robed in 13 Old Square and was walking briskly through the Inn, head in air for the benefit of some American tourists, my wig was suddenly snatched off my head by an overhanging branch of wisteria. I have never felt more foolish, standing there trying to reach back my wig, dangling as it was in mid-air.

CHAPTER 10

Marriage
King Henry's Road: August 1960

I SPENT SUNDAYS with Jenny in her house in Belsize Park, where I was thoroughly spoilt. Frequently the other girls were away at the weekends and we had the house to ourselves. Sometimes when it was too late for me to catch the last Underground train to Tufnell Park I walked back, a couple of miles, through the empty streets. London was a much safer place then.

We became engaged on Jenny's birthday in October 1959. I earned enough money for an engagement ring by revising the index for a new edition of Prideaux, a hefty book of conveyancing precedents. Payment for work done by barristers was notoriously slow in coming, and even in those early days I often waited for months, sometimes a year or more.

We were married the following year on 27th August in Ashton-under-Lyne at the church of St Michael and All Angels. This was a grade I listed church with 16th-century stained glass windows depicting the story of Old King Cole. The

With Jenny in Anglesey.

unusual square box pews meant that some of the wedding guests had to sit, rather uncomfortably, with their backs to the altar and the pulpit.

The rain held off until after the marriage service had ended and then it was torrential and went on and on. My father attended the service with Marjorie but managed to get lost afterwards and never found his way to Bank House, Jenny's home, where the reception was held. Many relations and friends travelled from London for the occasion, and a tight timetable was arranged for those who wished to return by train on the same day. Jenny's bridesmaids were her sister Gaynor, a doctor who specialised in anaesthetics, and her old Girton friend Hilary Wallace. Hilary practised as a solicitor in Newcastle-upon-Tyne. My supporter ('best man') was Peter Bentley.

After the reception we were driven across the moors to Buxton for two nights. Jenny was covered in confetti but the rain was too heavy for us to stop the car and let her get out for a moment to shake her clothes. But that did not matter because the linoleum floor-covering in the hotel bathroom had a confetti pattern. We holidayed in Doune, Scotland, and returned to London on the Flying Scotsman to our newly-rented furnished semi-basement flat in King Henry's Road, near Primrose Hill. Our kind Chinese landlady had filled the flat with flowers. We lived on Jenny's earnings and saved my scholarship money.

At Christmas in the following year we started house hunting.

Jenny and her parents on the moors.

CHAPTER II

By Another River
Stoke D'Abernon: Autumn 1962

MY FIRST FORAY was on a foggy day in early January 1962, when Jenny had returned to her work at the Gas Council after the Christmas break and I was still on vacation. We had been recommended Muswell Hill as a cheaper district than Hampstead Heath and Highgate. There I found a seemingly attractive house. On the next Saturday, full of hope, we returned briskly to Muswell Hill. As we walked up the hill I was amazed and appalled to see that, previously hidden by the thick fog, was the bulky structure of Alexandra Palace ('Ally Pally') looming over 'my' house. That was the end of our visits to Muswell Hill.

From then on, through the winter and into the spring, we spent every Saturday exploring the outskirts of London for a house which was affordable and suitable. We walked and walked and became very fit. One Saturday, on our way home, we chanced to find ourselves in Stoke D'Abernon on our way to the station. We glanced up Blundel Lane, an agreeable road, and a 'For Sale' notice on a house called Meadows aroused our interest.

Although not an architectural beauty the house enjoyed an attractive setting. The road wound gently uphill, and a cricket field and recreation ground with a line of ancient oaks lay immediately behind the house. At the far side of the recreation ground was a railway cutting, masked by more trees. Beyond that grazing cows added a rural touch to the overall scene. More importantly, indeed essentially because we had no car, the house was within easy walking distance of a station and a row of shops. The train journey to Waterloo was barely half an hour, which was the length of time we had set for ourselves as the maximum train travelling time. This was the 'loop' line from Waterloo to Guildford, as distinct from the older and more direct main line which ran some miles away through Weybridge and Woking.

We bought Meadows without ever seeing inside one of the bedrooms. The seller's mother used this room and kept the door locked except when she was in the house. Her presence in the house never coincided with our visits.

We came to know and have much affection for Stoke D'Abernon with its ancient church. The unusual place name is a combination of the original Saxon name

'Stocke' and the surname of Sir Roger D'Abernoun. He was rewarded with land in Surrey for his services to William the Conqueror. The church, St Mary's, was built in the late 7th or early 8th century and substantial portions of the original building still survive. It is one of the churches built immediately following St Augustine's introduction of Christianity to southern England in 597. The church stands in the grounds of the manor house, on the banks of the river Mole and surrounded by fields. The manor house is used today as a school and is now within the M25 circuit. On the other side of the river is the Yehudi Menuhin music school, established by the famous violinist in 1963.

We moved to Meadows in the autumn of 1962. Our journeys to work became longer, but they were still reasonable: mine was about an hour from door to door, Jenny's rather more.

Our first winter in Stoke was the bitterly cold one of 1962/1963. We spent Christmas in Beaumaris, Anglesey, visiting Jenny's parents and her father's family. When we returned to our new home we had a cold welcome. Everything in the house including the pipes was frozen. There was no central heating and the coal fire grates were small. The plumber lit the gas oven in the kitchen in an attempt to raise the temperature and I sought to unfreeze the bath taps by pouring boiling water over them. The plumber was successful but all I succeeded in doing was taking a huge chip out of the bath enamel. I spent the next five years trying to make good the damage.

In the spring of 1963 Jenny gave up her job with the Gas Council when she was expecting our first child. She had much pleasure in describing her status on a national insurance form as 'permanently retired'. John was born on 30th November and Gillian two years later, on 26th November 1965.

Our basic kitchen accessories were gradually augmented by gifts from Jenny's parents: a refrigerator when John was born, a washing machine when Gill was born. An aunt gave Jenny money for a fur coat but she used this to buy a dishwasher. Shortly before Gill was born we acquired our first car, a Vauxhall, second hand from Denis Chetwood, a member of 13 Old Square. Until then we were dependent on public transport and walking. In 1966, when the football world cup finals took place in England, I hired a television set for a month.

While living in Stoke we made many neighbour friends when we took turns attending St Mary's church or when pushing a pram to the local playground, or as we walked to Ash Ford and played on the banks of the river Mole, never quick enough to spot one of the kingfishers.

The rector at that time, John Waterson, attracted a large congregation and his church was very alive. We became quite involved. Jenny was a member of the parochial church council and the donations committee and helped for many years with unpopular jobs such as delivering the church magazine every month. For some years I was a churchwarden and also one of the lesson readers.

John Waterson did much to beautify and improve the interior of St Mary's: collecting old stained glass for the windows, installing a beautiful statue of Mary and the infant Jesus by the chancel step, hanging a fine picture of the Annunciation over the altar (later stolen), redecorating the walls and ceiling, acquiring handsome new staves for the wardens, and much more. He was keen on music and had a fine tenor voice, no doubt trained at his college, King's College, Cambridge. He masterminded

Jenny's sister Gaynor with John in 1965.

the purchase of a Frobenius organ. Members of the congregation, of whom I was one, excavated foundations for its installation at the west end of the nave.

The rector had strong views on many matters. One was an aversion to the Old Testament. At matins and evensong, instead of having one lesson from each testament, as was customary, his practice was to have one lesson from the New Testament and then a reading from a book (*The Fourth Lesson*) which comprised a collection of writings from outside the Bible. The bishop of Guildford came to hear of this, and the lesson readers were summoned to the rectory to meet him and the rector. Presumably the bishop's intention was to persuade the rector, and us, to mend our heretical ways. Needless to say, John Waterson remained unmoved and nothing changed.

CHAPTER 12

On The Hill
Cobham: February 1969

BY AUTUMN 1968 we were beginning to feel cramped with two growing children and moved across the parish boundary to a larger house in neighbouring Cobham. At this time a buyers' market was extant in the house property field, and we were able to upgrade without too much pain, finally moving in February 1969.

Christopher, our third child, was born in 1971 on the feast day of St Valentine, which coincided with 'decimalisation' day. Sadly, although Jenny's mother saw photographs of our new home, she was never able to come. We all enjoyed the visits her father was able to make on several occasions.

Leigh Hill Road is a contoured, wooded road about three-quarters of a mile long with a hill towards one end. In the 1960s it was a very different road from what it is today. Then there were four or five mansions, each with grounds of a couple of acres and each with its own entrance lodge. Additionally, and rather like poor men at the rich man's gate, there were about a dozen smaller houses with gardens of one-third of an acre. It was into one of these we moved. For this house, built in the mid-1930s in the style of a Surrey farmhouse with hanging tiles, our predecessors had chosen the rather twee name of 'Little Blakeney' after Blakeney, the village on the north Norfolk coast. I often wished I had changed the name when we first bought the house.

At this time there were open fields nearby, with grazing horses, and other large houses tucked out of sight up winding drives. Since then 'infilling' has never ceased. Groups of houses of varying sizes have replaced the mansions. The open fields have gone. The presence of the American Community School draws buyers of large houses, and the location of the training grounds of the Chelsea football club in Stoke D'Abernon also attracts wealthy players who are required to live close at hand. Whenever a house becomes vacant it is promptly demolished and replaced by a three-storey house with a small garden and seemingly innumerable bedrooms and bathrooms. Every month or two I receive an unsolicited letter from yet another estate agent breaking the news to me, as if I did not know, that my house and garden are ripe for redevelopment. Now the grassy slopes of Leigh Hill, covering the site of a Roman fort, are the only reminder that a century ago this was all one large area of open sandy heath.

CHAPTER 13

Making Progress
A Red Bag

ALL LAWYERS NEED tools. The law is complex and detailed, necessarily so if it is to provide adequately for the complexities of modern life. Unlike other countries, whose basic law is to be found in a comprehensive code, English law has developed piecemeal over centuries of parliamentary enactment and court decisions. Moreover, it is not static. It continues to develop. However learned, no lawyer can carry all he needs in his own head.

Nowadays computers afford instant access to comprehensive websites. This is now taken for granted. In the pre-computer days books were an essential aid for practising barristers: textbooks, as an orderly guide to the legislation and judicial decisions, and the source documents themselves comprising volumes of statutes, statutory instruments and reports of judicial decisions. These were needed as an aid when looking up a particular point of law or practice and also in order to keep abreast of continuing changes and developments in the law. When I started in practice, for instance, the current *Weekly Law Reports* were essential reading.

When I joined chambers in the late 1950s the facilities in 13 Old Square were rudimentary. There was no library, scarcely any text books, two or three sets of law reports in individual barristers' rooms and one or two copies of the 'White Book', so called because of the colour of its cover and containing the procedural rules of the High Court and Court of Appeal.

Perforce I constantly had resort of the well-equipped libraries in the Inns of Court. The Middle Temple was not conveniently placed for a practitioner on the far side of the Strand. I used the library in Lincoln's Inn so frequently I think the staff took it for granted I was a member of that Inn.

Gradually I bought one or two text books of my own. These could be expensive. The 'White Book', for instance, two volumes and later three, was published afresh every year. Then, in the late 1960s, after Peter Oliver and Brian Dillon had both taken silk in 1965, the head of chambers, Tom Strangman QC, retired. He was a formidable cross-examiner, but apt to be sharp in consultation with his own clients, both lay and professional. I bought his set of law reports and statutes, many hundreds of bound volumes. With the reshuffle of rooms in chambers consequent upon his retirement I acquired a room capable of holding all these books.

Law reports have a long history. There is not now, and never has been, an 'official' reporter. Reporting judicial decisions has been left to private enterprise. In England and Wales, starting with the 'Year Books' in the days of Edward II, a succession of individual reporters have attended the higher courts and prepared reports of decisions on points of law or practice, the earliest in legal Latin. Until the mid-19th century the quality of these reports was variable. One early reporter was said to listen to only half a case and then report the other half. In 1865 a non-profit making company, the Incorporated Council of Law Reporting, was set up with the object of publishing professionally-prepared reports of decisions of the superior courts of England and Wales. Its members are barristers nominated by the Inns of Court and the Bar Council. *The Law Reports* and the *Weekly Law Reports* published by this company are acceptable in all courts. Each report bears the initials of the reporter, and each reporter is a qualified barrister. Unlike other sets of reports, *The Law Reports* includes a summary of counsel's arguments, thereby making clear the extent of the legal issues in contention.

In the Chancery Division, when I was counsel, the two or possibly three reporters allocated to the chancery courts were insufficient for a reporter to be present in each court. The practice was that at the outset of a case the reporter would ask counsel, 'Is there anything in this case?' meaning, 'Does this case raise a legal issue which should be reported?' Usually the answer was 'no', because most cases at that level – it was different in the House of Lords – did not raise a reportable legal issue. Whereupon the reporter slipped away to seek prey in another court.

Having instant access to a set of law reports and statutes in my own room was a big step forward. This was the aim of every young chancery barrister in those days. It was an enormous saving of time. My books were a handsome leatherbound set, a delight to behold and to handle, although expensive to bind each year. Some of the older volumes, from the 1860s, were in need of repair, and I spread the repair programme over several years.

Many years later I passed these reports to my son John when he too had become a practising barrister in 13 Old Square and I had gone onto the bench where I had the use of law reports, not leatherbound, provided by Her Majesty's government.

I also built up an adequate collection of leading text books, plus the 'White Book'. The only snag was that other members of chambers, welcome to borrow my books, frequently did not return them. This defeated the purpose for which I had bought these expensive items. So I kept the books I most used out of sight in drawers of my desk.

Another development occurred in the late 1960s. When I started at the Bar, junior counsel – an alternative name for practising barristers – habitually carried their robes to court in a 'blue bag'. This was a soft, capacious blue brocade bag embroidered with the barrister's initials. In fact I never had such a bag. Instead I used Jenny's bag embellished with her initials JMT. The practice also was that if junior counsel being led by a QC gave his leader notable assistance in the case the leader presented him with a similar bag, but red in colour. A red bag was quite a prized possession, visible as it was to everyone else in the robing room. I understand this practice has now died out.

In the late 1960s an interesting case which came my way concerned Scotch whisky. I was led by John Brightman QC, later Lord Brightman. In those days much whisky sold abroad, particularly in South America, was a mixture of Scotch whisky and local spirits. It was sold in bottles under a get-up falsely indicating it was Scotch whisky, that is, whisky distilled in Scotland. Usually the label on the bottle did not actually say 'Scotch Whisky' but it carried indicia, such as tartans, suggesting a Scottish origin. All too easily the label gave an unwary buyer the impression that the whisky in the bottle was Scotch.

Taking preventive action against local shopkeepers abroad achieved little or nothing. So the Scotch Whisky Association broke fresh ground in this area of the law by initiating court proceedings in England against companies which exported Scotch whisky in bulk for the purpose of being admixed locally and then bottled and sold in this misleading way. The proceedings were successful. After they were over John Brightman gave me a 'red bag'. This was a gratifying step forwards.

Slowly, as I became more experienced, more and more of my time was spent in court, nearly always in London but sometimes in a chancery court in the provinces. One such occasion was in court in Manchester, where I was led by Sydney Templeman QC, later Lord Templeman. On the morning the case was fixed for hearing we went to the court from our hotel and changed into our robes in a crowded robing room. After we had donned our gowns Sydney could not find his wig. 'I must have left it behind in the hotel,' he said. I suggested he should wear my wig and start the case, and I would go back to the hotel and retrieve his wig from his room.

So I took a taxi back to the hotel and rummaged through his cupboards and bags and, embarrassingly, those of his wife who had come with him for the trip. Search as thoroughly as I could I was unable to find the missing wig. Empty handed, I returned, to the court and went into the robing room to don my robes again.

At The Bar

By now the room was deserted and empty. Everyone had finished robing and they had all dispersed to the various courtrooms. Lo and behold, there was Sydney's wig, lying forlornly and all alone on one of the benches. I rerobed and put on his wig and made haste back to court. As I entered the courtroom I was just in time to hear the judge saying that, because it was such a hot day, we could all remove our wigs for the sake of comfort.

CHAPTER 14

A Longer Wig
Silk: Easter 1974

EARLY IN THE 1970s the piles of papers awaiting attention in my room began to get out of control. Raggett advised me to 'take silk' but I was hesitant to do so. Taking silk has always been something of a professional gamble. Eventually I accepted his advice as I felt I could not sustain the pressure of work indefinitely.

'Taking silk' is the colloquial expression for being appointed Queen's Counsel or, to use the formal title, one of 'Her Majesty's Counsel learned in the law'. This is a status conferred by the Crown by letters patent. It is intended to reflect professional merit. 'Silk', because the gown worn by a QC is made of silk. In court QCs sit in a front row 'within the bar' of the court. On formal occasions they wear a long 'full bottomed' wig.

The professional gamble was that, particularly in those days, QCs were subject to restrictions which made their services considerably more expensive than those of junior counsel. Most important was the restriction that a QC could not appear in court without a junior barrister, and the convention was that the junior's fee would be two thirds of the amount of his leader's fee. So QCs were retained only in the more important cases. Nor could a QC draft pleadings or other documents.

I took the plunge in December 1972 and made a formal application to the lord chancellor supported by references from two judges. In addition I had to write to all the chancery juniors who were senior to me in point of call to the Bar and tell them of my intention. Appointments were made annually by the lord chancellor with the benefit of advice ('soundings') from the heads of divisions and other judges and legal luminaries. The procedure is very different today.

The result of applications was announced each year on Maundy Thursday. My application failed, and to raise my spirits I went out and bought a colour TV. I renewed my application in the following year and this time I was successful. That was at Easter 1974. It was a great relief.

The swearing-in ceremony took place in the Moses room in the House of Lords. The room was very crowded. Jenny and John were present but, as the lord chancellor Lord Elwyn-Jones observed, there was no more space 'not even for one bulrush'.

Taking silk, with John and Gill.

In those days the practice was that in the afternoon the new silks, wearing their silk gowns and long wigs, paraded into each of the law courts in the Strand. One by one they were called by the individual judges to 'take your seat within the bar'. Gill, eight years old, sat at the front of the court of the vice-chancellor, Sir John Pennycuick. She behaved impeccably. The judge was so intrigued that he kept peeping over the top of his dais at this young fair-haired angel visiting his court. Little did he know that what was keeping her so good was the feel of the sugar lump she had secreted in one of the fingers of her blue gloves.

The transition in my work was slow, but I had a sufficient backlog to keep me going for some time. Then my work became more varied. Most of it was litigation. I had cases at all levels of courts and in many different areas of law: principally commercial disputes, but also cases on copyright, trademarks, patents, and tax. The tax cases, in which I appeared for the Inland Revenue, were a welcome change. Most of my cases centred on points of interpretation of documents. Very few gave rise to points of law. Tax cases were an exception.

Overseas cases were interesting departures from the normal daily round. Many Commonwealth countries have inherited from England its common law and its legal procedures. The larger and more developed countries such as Canada and

Australia established their own legal professions a long time ago, but others were still doing so in the 1970s. So English barristers, particularly silks, were welcome and were called to the local bars in these countries to present cases there. On this basis I made several visits to Singapore and The Bahamas. Sometimes on visits to The Bahamas, as well as in London, I was instructed by the now legendary FA (Francis) Mann of Herbert Smith, whose renowned book, *Mann on the Legal Aspect of Money*, I had read and admired as an undergraduate.

On an advisory basis I also travelled to places as far apart as New York and Dublin. On the Dublin trip I had some spare time. In default of anything more attractive I went to a horse show outside the city. This did no more than confirm my antipathy to these shows. As a boy I had been bored at bank holiday agricultural shows at Willaston, Wirral. For me nothing had changed and I never went to another.

In November 1975 the secretary of state for trade appointed an accountant, Kenneth Wright, and me to investigate the affairs of a small company, Larkfold Holdings. He practised in the city of London and was a former president of the Institute of Chartered Accountants. There was nothing unusual about this investigation except that the principal witness was in Australia. This witness could not be compelled to come to London for questioning and so we had to travel to Sydney to interview him. Before we went we checked he was willing to see us and answer our questions.

At our own expense we flew by Concorde to Bahrain and then, at the government's expense, completed our journey at a more normal speed. Concorde was an exciting experience but the flight had its disconcerting moments: the hull of the plane became distinctly hot, and when the 'speedometer' in the main cabin failed to register the plane's supersonic speed the remedy was simply to give it a hefty thump.

Our trip to Sydney proved to be an appalling waste of time and money. Despite what had been arranged in writing the witness declined to give evidence save on unacceptable terms. We returned via Perth where I was fascinated to see some trot racing, and Cape Town where I was able to visit Peter Penny at his home.

In 1977, during a Labour government, one piece of highly contentious legislation concerned nationalisation of some parts of the aerospace and shipbuilding industries. The Bill had a stormy passage through Parliament. It was strenuously opposed by the Conservative opposition and rejected three times by the House of Lords. One notorious incident was when Michael Heseltine seized the mace in the House of Commons and, so the reports go, brandished it towards the Labour MPs as they sang the Red Flag to celebrate their success.

Companies and individuals most affected by this legislation then started proceedings in the European Court of Human Rights in Strasbourg, claiming that the compensation scheme breached several articles of the European Convention of Human Rights.

By the time these proceedings reached fruition the government had changed, following the 1979 general election. So the Conservative government found itself in the awkward position of having to defend in court the propriety of legislation to which the self-same Conservatives had objected so vehemently when in opposition.

Assisted by several juniors I was briefed on behalf of the government. The government was anxious to make sure my submissions did not give rise to any unnecessary embarrassment. So, before going to Strasbourg, I had to prepare my submissions for vetting by Downing Street. This was the only time a client asked to see my submissions in advance.

The case lasted several days. The government team, comprising four counsel and a like number of officials (civil servants), stayed at a hotel in the centre of Strasbourg. Each evening I was kept busy preparing my final submission while the officials were able to enjoy themselves exploring the city. On Friday evening, after the case had finished, everybody bolted back to London, leaving behind only myself and my erstwhile student Rosalyn Higgins, formerly Cohen. On Saturday morning she introduced me to the interesting parts of Strasbourg, and we then returned to the hotel to collect our belongings and leave. There a rude shock awaited me. I was known in the hotel as leader of the team, and the hotel presented me with a horrendous bill. Fortunately my newly acquired American Express card was equal to the occasion.

By the early 1980s I was ready for a change. I had been a practising barrister, arguing cases at every level of courts, for some twenty-five years. I had tried my hand at a variety of subjects. This had been very interesting, at times absorbing, but also quite demanding. Advocacy involves persuasion, persuading a judge to accept submissions. In a complex and difficult case this can be hard going. Further, a barrister must maintain his standards of preparation and presentation: in the eyes of instructing solicitors a barrister is only as good as his last case. And the higher your standards, the more solicitors expect from you.

Increasingly I had a sense of déjà vu. I had lost some of my appetite for yet another case: 'hardening of the arteries', as it is known in the profession. So it was a relief and delight, as well as an honour, when in July 1983 Lord Hailsham of St Marylebone, lord chancellor and head of the judiciary, offered me an appointment as a High Court judge in the Chancery Division.

On The Bench

CHAPTER 15

Red Robes And A Different Wig
High Court Bench: October 1983

THE SUMMER OF 1983 was a busy time. I had to wind down my practice without delay; we were engaged in extending the house in Cobham; all five of us went off on a Swan Hellenic cruise around the Mediterranean for a fortnight and, to make everything a little more complicated, I contrived to catch a dose of hepatitis. But we got through what was an exciting summer.

I was sworn in by Lord Hailsham in his room in the House of Lords on 30th September 1983, with Jenny and Gill and Christopher present. The two children were fascinated by his little white Jack Russell terrier. John was away playing football for Cambridge University on tour in Washington DC. I bought the scarlet robes and long judicial wig of my predecessor Mr Justice Foster. He was a very tall man and his robes were always too long for me. On the few occasions I wore them I had to take care not to trip over. Ordinarily I wore in court the same black gown and court coat as a QC.

On 4th October I took my seat for the first time in court in the Royal Courts of Justice in the Strand. Following the usual practice in the Chancery Division I was welcomed with short speeches from a QC and a junior barrister in the presence of other counsel and solicitors. By now John had returned from his football trip. By a happy chance Peter Bentley was in London and was there as well.

Appointment to the High Court bench carries with it a knighthood. Surprisingly and disappointingly the visit to the palace takes the form of a private audience with the Queen. So Jenny was not able to attend. In my case the Queen was abroad, and it was the Queen Mother and Princess Margaret who 'officiated'. Contrary to what I had been told in advance the Queen Mother did actually say 'Arise, Sir Donald'. Which I suspect would not have been said by the Queen.

I then began hearing cases. I had sat a few times as a deputy High Court judge, so the experience was not entirely novel. I was of course familiar with the procedures and the nature of the work, but some features came as a surprise. I was surprised to find how lonely I was. Each judge was fully occupied with his own cases, so during the day I met nobody except my clerk. Most days I lunched in my Inn, but quite

High Court judge, with Jenny, Gill and Christopher.

often I worked in my room in the lunch break, preparing notes for a judgment to be given in the afternoon or looking up some point counsel had not presented adequately. I missed the comradeship of 13 Old Square.

I was also taken aback by the non-stop nature of the work. The clerk of the lists was, rightly, concerned with the length of time many parties to cases had to wait before they could be heard by a judge. His aim was to keep every judge busy throughout each day. As counsel I was accustomed to going into court to present just one case at a time. Now, as soon as I finished one case I started another, day after day after day. I did not always have as much time to prepare as I would have wished.

One of my cases concerned the interpretation of a will. The solicitors later turned the case into this advertisement, warning others against the risk of having to appear in court before me if their wills were homemade:

‘A few days before her death Mrs Enid Williams made a will. She wrote it herself. After her death her executors could not distribute her estate because

With John.

they could not understand her will. The executors applied to the High Court for help. So, in December 1984, no less than six barristers stood before Mr Justice Nicholls in London to ask for a ruling. DON'T LET YOUR FAMILY AND FRIENDS END UP LIKE THOSE OF MRS WILLIAMS.'

The solicitors then distributed this advertisement from house to house in their locality. The amusing twist is that the solicitors' office was in Cobham and one letterbox through which they pushed this flyer was mine.

I heard some interesting cases. Several of them found their way into newspaper cartoons, a practice which seems now to have died out. One of them concerned a dispute between well-known personalities: Elton John and his lyricist Bernie Taupin on the one hand and the music publisher Dick James on the other. The trial extended over fifty working days. Elton John gave evidence, and the press could not resist a cartoon showing him playing an imaginary grand piano in court and singing his oath: 'I swear to tell the truth, the whole truth and nothing but the truth. So help

Elton John cartoon.

me G-o-o-o-o-o d.' Robed counsel provided the backing ('Do-be-do-do-wah'), and I am shown admonishing Elton John: 'Er… just READ the card, Mr John, thank you very much.'

Sometime later a case concerning Tottenham Hotspur football club came before me. The chief executive Terry Venables and the chairman Alan Sugar had fallen out, and Venables' service contract had been ended. The application before me was for a temporary order preserving Terry Venables' position as manager. One cartoon showed a robed barrister addressing the judge: 'who, M'Lud, will want to own a football club if they can't have the fun of sacking the manager?'

Venables was popular with the club's supporters. I received over 700 supportive letters. Many fans turned up at the Royal Courts of Justice to express their support in person. They demonstrated in the Strand with placards such as 'One man's money versus 27,000 people's wishes.' The police herded them behind crush barriers and onto the island in the middle of the Strand beside St Clement Danes church (of 'Oranges and Lemons' fame). The proceedings were heard in the biggest courtroom in the Royal Courts of Justice.

When I was about to give judgment I became concerned at the likelihood of a demonstration in the court room if, as I was proposing to decide, Venables would not be continuing as the team manager. In order to avoid any unseemly behaviour I couched my judgment in opaque language:

> 'I shall therefore not make any order as asked. I shall rise now for a few moments and sit again to hear any applications there may be regarding costs or other ancillary matters.'

I then scuttled out of court, as quickly as judicial dignity permitted, before any trouble could break out.

Next day the press seized on this as the subject of a cartoon. I was shown dancing and waving a Spurs' scarf while an elderly supporter is asking a policeman, 'Excuse me, officer, is the judge chanting Sugar or Venables?' Brandon Jackson, by now the dean of Lincoln, sent me a postcard: 'I know why you did it – you want him for Tranmere Rovers.'

In September 1984 I was the 'new boy' among the chancery judges and was sitting as vacation judge. At that time the 1984–85 miners' strike was at its height. Some miners from Derbyshire and Yorkshire did not wish to join in the strike. They brought proceedings against the National Union of Mineworkers and its president Mr Arthur Scargill. The defendants did not appear in court, and when I had read the papers and heard the submissions I ruled that the NUM had breached

FRANKLIN

SOCCER
COURT
CASE

" EXCUSE ME, OFFICER, IS THE JUDGE CHANTING SUGAR OR VENABLES?"

Terry Venables cartoon.

its own constitution by calling a strike without first holding a ballot. The miners were lawfully entitled to disregard instructions to strike.

These events were headline news in all the newspapers. Arthur Scargill's response, as reported in the press, was that my decision represented 'another attempt by an unelected judge to interfere in the affairs of an independent and democratic trade union.' This led to a pertinent cartoon of a barrister saying in court, 'My client is not in court, m'lud, but he will be making a statement on Channel Four this evening.' Mr Scargill disregarded the orders I had made, and the non-striking miners returned to court. Again the defendants did not appear in court. I adjourned the proceedings for a few days to enable the NUM and Arthur Scargill to reflect further on their position and to reconsider the desirability of being represented at the adjourned hearing. The front-page news item in the evening newspapers was 'Scargill – time to reflect' and 'Six days to think'. This was party conference time. Arthur Scargill was attending the Labour party's conference at Blackpool and he was served with

Arthur Scargill cartoon.

the court papers while he was there. This led to a cartoon depicting him sitting at the conference, in a pose reminiscent of Rodin's statue *Le Penseur*, with some colleagues nearby looking at him and saying 'Sometimes, Arthur sits and thinks … and sometimes he just sits'. A large cartoon in the *Daily Mail* showed me sitting in my room in the law courts reading a newspaper article headed 'Scargill deadline looms'. Several judges had come into my room and one of them was saying to me, 'We've been thinking Donald – why not sentence him to a couple of days at the Tory conference without police protection?'

At the adjourned hearing I pointed out that a large and powerful trade union had regarded itself as above the law and was bent on saying to its members and the whole nation that it was untouchable. I fined the NUM £200,000 for contempt of court and Arthur Scargill £1,000. His fine was paid anonymously, but the NUM did not pay its fine. Its assets were sequestered (seized by the court).

Many months later Arthur Scargill and his co-officials came into my court and applied for the sequestration order to be lifted. When the court usher came into my room to announce the court was ready she said the court was packed, with 'standing room only'. 'But', she added, turning to me with a smile, 'I have kept a seat for you.' In December 1985, to my utter amazement I was offered an appointment as a lord justice in the Court of Appeal. This was very much a bolt out of the blue. I had been a judge for little more than two years.

CHAPTER 16

Black And Gold Robes
Court of Appeal: February 1986

A LITTLE KNOWN fact, which I shall mention first, is that by longstanding convention judges of the Court of Appeal are appointed members of the Queen's own council ('Privy Council'). The formal title is Her Majesty's Most Honourable Privy Council.

The council has a long history of advising the sovereign, and it usually meets at Buckingham Palace about once a month. A feature of these meetings is that the Queen normally remains standing throughout, so that the members may not sit down, thereby keeping meetings short. Reputedly this practice originated with Queen Victoria.

Today there are about 500 members: past and present members of the cabinet, archbishops, leaders of all major political parties and senior judges. There is no question of all these members being invited to the meetings. The whole council is convened rarely, for instance, following the death of the monarch. In the ordinary course meetings are attended by several ministers to seek the Queen's formal approval to a number of orders already approved by them. The procedure is much the same as statutes becoming law through the giving of the royal assent after the Bills have been debated and approved in Parliament.

The ceremony of becoming a member of the council involves swearing a lengthy oath, of which I had no prior knowledge, and kissing the Queen's hands. In contrast to the elaborate letters patent issued on judicial appointments, the only documentation produced to mark this occasion for me was the copy of the New Testament on which I took my oath of allegiance with a label inside, signed by the lord president of the council, recording that I was 'sworn of Her Majesty's Most Honourable Privy Council' on 26th March 1986. This is the only council meeting judges normally attend. So, except for one matter to which I shall come later, the appointment is purely honorific for judges. They, like other privy councillors, are entitled to use the prefix 'Right Honourable'.

Self-evidently there is one fundamental difference between the work of an appeal court judge and the work of a trial judge ('a judge of first instance' or a 'puisne' judge, meaning a junior judge). When a case reaches the Court of Appeal a judge of first instance has already heard the witnesses and counsel's arguments ('submissions') and given his decision. In the Court of Appeal the question is whether the judge's decision was right. (I am confining myself to civil cases and say nothing about criminal cases tried by a judge and jury.)

This difference dictates a major procedural difference: judges in the appeal court do not rehear cases from scratch; they do not hear evidence from witnesses in the witness box. In the Court of Appeal cases proceed on the basis of the evidence heard by the trial judge, and this evidence is presented to the Court of Appeal in the form of transcripts.

A further difference is that the appeal court judges have the benefit of the decision of the judge of first instance. Appropriately, while a puisne judge sits alone, the appeal court judges usually sit in groups of three, all of whom have previous experience as trial judges. This ensures that at least two experienced judges must disagree with the trial judge before his decision can be reversed.

Another, less obvious difference is that judges of first instance normally hear cases in their own specialist fields, for example, family law, but in the Court of Appeal lords justices sit on cases across the whole spectrum of legal work. So decisions of the Court of Appeal are the product of the collective experience of three judges, often having different professional backgrounds. Inherently their decisions should be more reliable than those of a single judge sitting alone. They can learn from one another.

Another and important difference is that judges in the Court of Appeal hear a higher proportion of heavier cases, 'heavier' in the sense that the factual and legal issues are more complex and difficult. The more straightforward cases do not normally reach the Court of Appeal. This makes the work more interesting. The disadvantage for the appellate judges is that counsel's submissions in the cases take longer and more judgments have to be reserved, that is, not given immediately at the close of counsel's submissions. Reserved judgments, to which I shall return in a moment, have to be considered and written in the evenings or at weekends or in the vacations, and this adds substantially to a judge's workload. The Court of Appeal is renowned for having the heaviest workload of all courts.

In short, moving into the Court of Appeal involved entering a more communal and more high-powered world with a heavier workload.

Time spent by judges in court, with attendant counsel and solicitors, is highly expensive for the lay clients. At the end of the case one or other of the parties has to pay the costs of the other side's solicitors and barrister as well as their own. In order to minimise time spent in court by counsel reading aloud documents such as correspondence, which could equally well and probably more quickly be read

At House of Lords being sworn in for Court of Appeal.

by a judge for himself in his own room, Lord Donaldson, when master of the rolls, introduced a system of 'reading' days. One day each week the lords justices did not sit in court. Instead they stayed behind the scene in their own rooms and read the papers, often voluminous, provided in advance for the following week's cases, aided by a synopsis of each counsel's submissions. These synopses were intended to be concise, 'skeleton arguments' they were called, but as time passed they tended to become ever more longwinded.

Undoubtedly this system did save court time, although the barristers often fretted at the inconvenience, even difficulty, of producing definitive skeleton arguments some weeks before the trial was due to start.

These reading days became a boon for the judges in a way Lord Donaldson perhaps had not foreseen. I soon found, and I was not alone in this, that reading days were much more valuable when treated as 'writing' days. Reading documents and skeleton arguments in advance could often be fitted into short slots of time as and when they became available, for instance, in the evenings. Writing a judgment called, preferably, for a prolonged period of time in which to think and draft without interruption. For this the reading days were ideal.

I worked at home on these reading days whenever practicable. I had fewer interruptions and was more relaxed. The children knew I should not be disturbed. On one occasion Gill, still a young girl, tried to quieten some noise in the hall. 'Hush,' she said, 'Daddy is sleeping in his study.'

Cases reaching the Court of Appeal were of importance to one or both of the parties. However important, in most cases the decision of the Court of Appeal was final. There was no further appeal. The law lords concentrated their attention on appeals raising legal questions of general public importance: they were only able to hear about seventy appeals each year. Very few decisions of the Court of Appeal satisfied that criterion.

Although important to the parties, appeals in the Court of Appeal were usually of little or no general interest. They do not bear repetition. This was not always so, and I give an example of an interesting, run of the mill appeal I heard in the Court of Appeal which was factually and legally straightforward. My fellow lords justices hearing the appeal were Brian Dillon, an outstandingly able chancery lawyer, and Fred Lawton, a highly experienced criminal lawyer with an abundance of common sense.

The case concerned a field of wild oats in Essex. The claimant was an arable farmer who had sown winter wheat on 600 acres of his land. That was in the autumn of 1982. In the following spring he needed to kill the weed known as wild oats which was growing in the crop. For this purpose he bought some herbicide from a firm of agricultural suppliers. On the back of the cans the instructions for use stated expressly the crop stages within which alone application of the herbicide was recommended: the user should 'stop spraying' after these growth stages were reached.

As it happened, the spring of 1983 was cold and wet, so much so there never was a time when the weather was warm enough and the land dry enough for the weed killer to be used until after the 'stop spraying' limit had passed. Despite this, the farmer sprayed the herbicide, taking a risk on damage to his crops, because he wanted to destroy the wild oats, and in particular to avoid the possibility that the wild oats would seed over his land and infest his crop in the following year.

Unfortunately the herbicide did virtually no good, and the farmer sued the suppliers for breach of contract. The herbicide, he said, was not fit for the purpose for which it was sold.

The claim succeeded in front of the trial judge, but not in the Court of Appeal. The reason why the weed killer failed was that it was sprayed too late. An important feature of this herbicide was that, after spraying, the wheat continues to grow and smothers the weed. When there is little further crop growth, as happened in the present case, the herbicide is substantially less effective.

The trial judge upheld the farmer's claim, on the basis that the instructions for use were misleading. In the Court of Appeal we took a different view. The instructions set out clearly the period within which spraying should take place. So the appeal succeeded and the farmer's claim failed.

Apart from the incessant pressure of work the only real drawback in the Court of Appeal was the lack of adequate secretarial assistance. On this the court service lagged behind the times. Each judge was provided with a 'clerk'. The clerk was in the nature of a personal valet. This may have been appropriate for judges who went out of London on circuit and stayed in judges' lodgings for days or weeks on end. The requirements of chancery judges and lords justices were different. They needed a personal secretary. Those were still the days of typewriters, before the arrival of computers. Professional men were not trained to type nor were they accustomed to doing so. Judges whose work kept them in London needed an assistant who could type a reserved judgment, with reasonable expedition, in a state fit for handing down to the parties. This was not a role for which the clerks were fitted, even though they did their best with two fingers.

Judges in the Court of Appeal wore rather grand robes for ceremonial occasions such as the annual service in Westminster Abbey at the start of the legal year. The robes were covered in gold braid with an ornate train borne by an usher. When wearing their long wigs they were well and truly disguised. All you could see was the front of the face, not unlike a hijab.

Judicial robes have undergone changes since 2008. In my day, when sitting in court lords justices wore the same black robes as a chancery judge with wing collars and bands (strips of linen hanging down the front of the neck) and a short bench wig. Even this short wig can be effective to conceal identity. On one occasion, after I had been sitting in court all day as a single judge, I walked out and crossed the Strand to the bus stop. I soon realised, from what a couple standing beside me in the queue were saying, that they had been present in my court all day but had not recognised me.

Whether this is a good argument in favour of judges wearing wigs I very much doubt. Judges all over the world, and many judges in this country, manage satisfactorily without the visual disguise afforded by 18th-century male headdress. A little later, when I was vice-chancellor, I chaired a meeting of chancery judges who voted in favour of abolishing wigs. The commercial judges were of the same view, but other judges, particularly the criminal judges, thought differently, so nothing changed.

Three unexpected honours came my way after my promotion to the Court of Appeal: the governors of Birkenhead School appointed me president of the school; Liverpool University admitted me to the 'Degree of Doctor of Laws (honoris causa)' and the master and fellows of Trinity Hall elected me as an honorary fellow of the college. I greatly appreciated each of these honours which cemented further my links with these excellent institutions.

Throughout my first year in the Court of Appeal I continued to travel daily on the train to and from Cobham. With an increased workload and more evening commitments I began to feel the need to cut down on the time spent travelling. At Easter 1987 I was fortunate to obtain a lease of a flat belonging to the Middle Temple. The demand for barristers' chambers in the Inn exceeded supply, but the top floors in the Inn's buildings were still used by residential tenants. This was in conformity with the City of London's planning policy of retaining some residents in the City.

I acquired a lease of the third floor of Devereux Chambers, reached by 66 steps. There was no lift, but that did not deter us. The two living rooms in the flat had an agreeable view over Fountain Court and Middle Temple hall, with a glimpse of the Inn garden and the river Thames. The fountain dates from 1681. It was immortalised in 1843 by Charles Dickens, who was a member of the Inn, in his novel *Martin Chuzzlewit*:

'Brilliantly the Temple fountain sparkled in the sun, and laughingly its liquid music played, and merrily the idle drops of water danced and danced, and peeping out in sport among the trees plunged lightly down to hide themselves, as little Ruth and her companion came towards it.'

The other rooms in the flat were improved by obscuring their outlook with net curtaining spread across the windows.

The flat proved to be a lifesaver, once we had made it ready for use with our own furnishings and decorations. I had a car parking facility in the law courts and, some years later, a parking space in the Inn. Normally I spent four nights in the flat each week during the law terms. When one of the boys was living there Jenny spent two nights in the flat, expanding to four nights after they had both moved elsewhere. She carried up the food and clothing and kept the flat under control as well as doing all the cooking. Often she went shopping for my jackets and trousers, even shoes, and returned them to the shops if unsuitable, because I was too busy to find time to visit the West End.

It was heavy going for her. She also bore the brunt of the driving especially when, at a much later stage, I had the use of a government car to bring me home on Thursday evenings from the House of Lords.

We kept the flat for twenty-five years, such was its usefulness as a London base. Although it was not acquired for the boys' use the flat proved to be a boon for them as well. John lived there with us for four years, Christopher for rather longer.

CHAPTER 17

Still Black And Gold
Vice-Chancellor: October 1991

IN OCTOBER 1991 I was appointed vice-chancellor of the Chancery Division. To understand this title and office a little history is necessary. Until 1875 a variety of courts administered different laws and sat in different places. The Court of Chancery, administering 'equity', was headed by the lord chancellor. This court sat in the southwest corner of Westminster Hall during term time (about three months in the year) and at other times in the Old Hall of Lincoln's Inn. As one critic said, 'The lord chancellor of England now sits, by sufferance, in a dining hall.' Several other courts, administering the 'common law' and headed by their own chief justices, sat in different parts of Westminster Hall, as did the judge of the probate and divorce courts and the judge of the High Court of Admiralty. Other courts, such as the Insolvent Debtors Court, and the judges' chambers and the masters' offices, were dispersed chaotically throughout London.

In 1875 the court system was reorganised and the multifarious courts were consolidated into one Supreme Court of Judicature (now known as the Senior Courts of England and Wales). Instead of being spread piecemeal around London, the new court was accommodated on a single site, in a complex of court rooms in a new purpose-built building: the Royal Courts of Justice on the north side of the Strand. To enable this to be done many small houses had to be demolished. Even today the site of one of the old narrow streets, Bell Yard, remains extant.

The Supreme Court of Judicature was created with two levels: the Court of Appeal, under the master of the rolls, and the High Court of Justice. The High Court had three divisions: the Chancery Division, under the lord chancellor; the Queen's Bench Division, under the lord chief justice; and the Probate Divorce and Admiralty division (wills, wives and wrecks), under the president. I need not elaborate on the later changes save to note that in about 1970 the senior judge in the Chancery Division was accorded the title of vice-chancellor. It was to this office, as the de facto head of the Chancery Division, I was appointed. At that time there were about a dozen chancery judges.

At my desk as Vice–Chancellor.

The principal difference between my work as a lord justice and as vice-chancellor was that, once again, I sat as a judge of first instance and, more significantly, I became involved in some administrative work. That was a novel experience for me. As head of the Chancery Division I chaired meetings of the chancery judges and was responsible for dealing with all manner of problems arising in the running of the division.

Additionally, and importantly, I participated in the monthly meetings of the heads of divisions with the lord chancellor. We met in his room in the House of Lords. These were small meetings, comprising the lord chancellor in the chair, his permanent secretary and the four heads of divisions. At that time the lord chancellor was still the head of the judiciary and responsible for most aspects of its functioning and administration. He was also a senior member of the cabinet. Further, although this carried no powers, he was the speaker of the House of Lords. So he had a multifarious role which, I have to say, was advantageous to the judiciary and the country as a whole. For he embodied, at the highest level, a minister who understood and supported the rule of law.

The system has now changed. Unlike other countries, separation of powers has never featured in the British constitution. To this day, the executive and the legislature are not separated. But the judiciary is now separated from the other arms of government so far as that can be done. Whether that separation was a wise step is open to debate, but I have no doubt that a secretary of state for justice who is not an experienced lawyer is at a grave disadvantage.

Meetings of heads of divisions covered a wide range of subjects: advising on problems affecting judges which had come before the lord chancellor and on which he wished to seek our views, and advising on appointments of High Court judges and lords justices and, once a year, QCs.

This appointments system did have advantages. In the case of judicial appointments some, if not all of us, knew the potential appointees. I believe the best way of assessing who would make a good judge or lord justice is to have sat with him or her on the bench or to have worked alongside him or her in practice or in some other way.

These meetings were very interesting although preparing for them, by reading and considering the agenda and papers thoroughly, could be very time-consuming.

Most chancery cases were tried in London but some in provincial centres. Manchester, Liverpool, Leeds and other cities in the north were the largest centres. One of the chancery judges, usually with northern connections, was appointed vice-chancellor of the County Palatine of Lancaster. He spent some months each year at these northern cities.

In addition chancery cases were tried in Birmingham, Bristol and Cardiff. These three centres were the responsibility of Circuit judges, formerly known as County Court judges, who had undertaken some chancery work while in practice as barristers. When I was vice-chancellor I decided to visit each of these three centres, to obtain a better insight into their work. So, accompanied by Jenny, I spent one week in each city, trying chancery cases. We stayed at the judges' lodgings. This was itself quite an experience, because this was my only acquaintance with circuit life. We met much kindness.

The upshot of my visits was that, at my request, the lord chancellor set up a small committee to investigate the work of these centres. I did not see the outcome because by then I had moved on.

One interesting surprise I had as vice-chancellor was to receive a letter from the president of Clare Hall, Cambridge, informing me that under the statutes of the college I was the visitor of the college. To be frank I was not even aware of the existence of this graduate college. In my defence I noted that the college was founded as recently as 1966. The president told me that, in the ordinary course, this office carried with it nothing more onerous than an expectation I would attend the college's annual principal feast with my wife. So I accepted my new responsibility. I was relieved to find that during my years as visitor nothing happened within the college calling for adjudication by me.

In 1993 the heads of divisions had an unusual engagement. The president of the Law Society, the solicitors' professional association, invited the four of us to attend as guests at the Society's forthcoming annual conference at Brighton. We were to constitute a 'brains trust' under the chairmanship of Sir Robin Day, the television journalist and political commentator. This invitation was difficult to refuse, even though there were obvious risks in responding impromptu, in front of a large professional audience, to prepared questions of which we would have no forewarning. So Lord Taylor, Sir Thomas Bingham, Sir Stephen Brown and I duly presented ourselves for our grilling.

Our fears proved to be unfounded. Robin Day was at his most gentle, and the conference was equally restrained and polite. One question, addressed to each of us, was: if you could change one thing in the present legal system, what would you change? My response was:

> If I could make one change I would take the White Book, all three volumes of it, and burn it. I would have the rules rewritten in a form anyone can understand. I would have orders drafted in a form people can understand and recognise as being in English. That would make an improvement in the administration of justice but also in the impression the consumer gets. Instead of thinking he is going into some strange world where people use language … people never use, he would actually be able to understand what was going on.

This answer went down well and was greeted with enthusiastic applause.

As a judge I naturally spent most of my working day in court. Of their nature proceedings in court are not a bundle of fun. This, self-evidently, is so with criminal cases. It is also true of civil cases because they are concerned with disputes whose outcome may matter greatly to one or both of the parties. In a less serious vein, on one occasion when I was a High Court judge a woman barrister came in front of me. She was obviously in an advanced stage of pregnancy, so I invited her to address me while seated. When his turn to address me came her opponent, a fit young barrister, rose to his feet. He asked if he too might remain seated while he made his submissions to me. What should I have said?

Behind the scenes I was surprised on another occasion when my clerk entered my room on his hands and knees, with one finger to his lips, beckoning me to follow him in the like posture. Which I did. When we reached his room the kestrel at his window had flown but looking down on us, unbelievingly, was another judge. 'How often do you do this?' he asked.

While I was in the Court of Appeal my clerk was a woman, also named Jennifer. She had been with me a very short time. One evening I reached up to the top shelf in my coat cupboard, and to my amazement I pulled down a cardboard box full of jewellery. When Jennifer next came into my room and saw the jewellery on my desk she said, 'So you have found Aladdin's cave. I thought you were too busy ever to look on the top shelf. None of my other judges did.'

CHAPTER 18

Best Bib And Tucker
Ceremonial Occasions

AT THE BEGINNING of October each year a judges' service was held in Westminster Abbey to mark the start of another legal year. The abbey was closed to the public for the occasion. The judges gathered in the nave, wearing their ceremonial robes. When the lord chancellor arrived he processed along the nave followed by the judges, in strict order of precedence, and then the new QCs and other lawyers. Meanwhile the wives and other visitors had been seated in the transepts, with the law lords wearing morning dress seated alongside the choir. The procession was lengthy and from beginning to end lasted fifteen to twenty minutes. So we were all allowed to sit until, eventually, the dean and the choristers came into sight and processed into the chancel.

Seated in the chancel, and even more so when seated next to the choir, the music was breathtaking. The services as a whole were impressive and uplifting.

After the service the judges left by a side door at the south corner of the abbey and processed across St Margaret's Street to the Palace of Westminster. The road had to be closed to traffic and pedestrians. Understandably, this was not popular.

In my early days the procession entered the palace at the peers' entrance and thence up to the royal gallery to be received there by the lord chancellor plus refreshments. More recently, as this annual service became the occasion for entertaining representatives of courts and legal bodies from Europe, the royal gallery could no longer accommodate everybody and so the procession was rerouted through St Stephen's entrance and into the more spacious Westminster Hall.

Originally the refreshments comprised a drink and nibbles. This was not altogether satisfactory because from this function the judges went back to the law courts and straight into court, without anything else to eat. When Lord Irvine of Lairg was lord chancellor the refreshments turned into a buffet lunch. Which was much better.

The wives were not invited to the reception. At the end of the abbey service Jenny and some of the other wives went off together to lunch somewhere interesting.

Another regular function was attending the state opening of Parliament by the Queen, usually once a year. The heads of divisions and a dozen or so judges, fully robed, sat on the woolsack, immediately in front of the Queen. As with all royal functions there was a lot of waiting. The compensation for the judges was that, before the hereditary peers were banished, the duchesses sat nearby in evening dress, with an abundance of twinkling tiaras and glittering jewellery. Some of them were very pretty.

The wives were able to apply for a ticket for a place in the royal gallery, through which the Queen processed to and from the chamber of the House of Lords. I say a ticket for a 'place' because in the early days there was no seating in the royal gallery, so Jenny had a very protracted stand. The alternative was to sit on the floor. More recently seating has been provided.

This was always a highly colourful occasion with an abundance of lavish ceremony. Everyone entitled to robes wore them. Those present included a liberal sprinkling of officers with grand titles, such as the lord great chamberlain and fitzroy pursuivant extraordinary, wearing suitably magnificent outfits. The heralds of the College of Arms, clad in their remarkable tabards, shuffled into the chamber at the last moment. By the time the Queen arrived all was set. The chamber was filled to overflowing with peers in their scarlet, bishops and judges in their robes, ambassadors in their national costumes, and wives in evening dress. When the Queen passed through the royal gallery and into the chamber, wearing the imperial state crown, she was preceded by the earl marshal walking backwards.

An interesting contrast was provided when Black Rod summoned the members of the House of Commons to attend the House of Lords to hear the 'Speech from the Throne' read by the Queen. The prime minister and other ministers and members of Parliament arrived noisily and stood at the bar of the House in ordinary day dress. 'Black Rod' is the serjeant-at-arms to the lord chancellor and derives his name from the colour of his rod of office.

The Queen's speech was written for her by the government, outlining its agenda for the coming year. The lord chancellor, wearing his elaborate gold robes and with lots of bowing, handed the speech to the Queen after mounting the steps to the throne and kneeling in front of her. He then walked away, backwards, down the steps. He repeated this manoeuvre to collect the script from the Queen after she had read the speech. These were always anxious moments in case the lord chancellor tripped on his long robes or missed his footing when walking backwards.

A different kind of ceremonial event was attending dinners in the City of London. Each year the lord mayor invites High Court judges, and those more senior, and their spouses to a dinner in the Mansion House. These were splendid 'white tie' occasions and highly enjoyable. The lord mayor similarly entertains the bishops each year. At one of the judges' dinners the wife of a former lord mayor remarked to me, in an unguarded moment, that the bishops' dinners were of course much more fun. The truth will out.

In November each year the lord mayor hosts the Lord Mayor's Banquet in the Guildhall. It is his first dinner in his year of office, in honour of the immediately past lord mayor. The heads of divisions, robed in all their finery, were invited to these dinners, with their wives wearing their most elaborate evening dresses. They were glittering occasions. The prime minister attended and delivered what was called 'the keynote address'. The wives had to take care not to snag their dresses on their husbands' gold braid.

The heads of divisions and their spouses were also invited to some of the dinners given by the lord mayor to heads of state on state visits. In November 1993 Jenny was laid low with a serious form of Bell's palsy. At two dinners held in that month, the Lord Mayor's Banquet for that year and the state visit of Yang Di-Pertuan Agong of Malaysia, Gill deputised for Jenny. She looked charming. One of the other guests was heard to observe that I had a very young wife.

On 24th November 1992 Jenny and I attended a memorable lunch at the Guildhall, marking the fortieth anniversary of the Queen's accession to the throne. During the year several matrimonial misfortunes had occurred within the royal family and then on 20th November Windsor Castle caught fire and was seriously damaged. In her speech the Queen observed that the year 'is not one on which I shall look back with undiluted pleasure … it has turned out to be an *annus horribilis*.'

To complete this round of social activities I should mention that the judges are also invited to one of the garden parties given each year by the Queen in the gardens of Buckingham Palace. These are attended by several thousand guests. When we first attended one of these parties the invitation included unmarried daughters but not other members of the family. So John missed out on the occasion. His participation was confined to acting as our chauffeur, although he did attend a party in his own right some years later after he had taken silk. In later years, no doubt mindful of sex discrimination, these invitations were extended to unmarried sons, and both Gill and Christopher attended parties in due course.

On these occasions the queues into the palace grounds were formidable and parking in the Mall was difficult. We were delighted to discover that members of the Privy Council, as well as ambassadors, could park their cars in Wellington Barracks on Birdcage Walk and use a side entrance to the palace. So no more queues. At a later stage we were honoured to be invited each year to join the Queen for tea in the royal tent.

CHAPTER 19

The Next Generation
Schools and Weddings

BY THE EARLY 1980s the children were growing up and needed education. Choosing schools is like choosing horses for courses. With the two boys we were fortunate, but less so with Gill.

When we began thinking about a school for John we were still new to the district. We knew nothing about any of the schools, which of them were good and to be sought and which were indifferent and to be avoided. Initially I was not averse to John going to the local state school close to hand, but I soon realised, from the experience of friends and neighbours, that the quality of teaching there was not so good as at some local fee-paying schools.

But how to choose? I have found that a useful source of advice about schools comes from the schools one further step up the educational ladder. So we went to see the headmasters at several post-prep schools. One of them, very kindly and most helpfully, responded 'yes' or 'no' when we named some of the local prep schools. With this guidance, and after visiting the school, we chose Danes Hill, Oxshott. It was then a small school of about one hundred boys. It is now a mixed school and one of the biggest preparatory schools in the country.

It was a happy decision. John flourished there. He was taught well, except in mathematics. He acquired a love of football, and captained the school's unbeaten football team. At home I kicked a football with him on the lawn or, after Christmas when the grass had been ruined, in the small wood at the foot of the garden. In the summer the other popular game was croquet.

John would have been head boy had he stayed at Danes Hill until he was thirteen, but Martin Scott, the second master at Winchester College, said it would be better to start at Winchester at the same time as the other new 'men', much to John's disappointment. David Calcutt, a barrister friend, later Sir David Calcutt, had pointed us firmly in the direction of Winchester.

This was sound guidance. In 1976 John took the election (scholarship) exam at Winchester. This lasted several days, and I stayed with him at a hotel in Winchester. Croquet hoops were laid out in the hotel garden, ready for play, so one evening we went to the hotel desk and asked if we could borrow two croquet mallets and balls. 'Croquet?' said the receptionist, handing us two golf putters and two golf balls, 'Whatever makes you think the hoops are for croquet?'

John was awarded a scholarship, and at Winchester he caught up on his maths and became prefect of hall (head boy). His unflagging enthusiasm and sheer determination enabled him to be a member of his school's football team.

Martin Scott taught him how to play bezique. This spread around the family and became a popular game at home. On the inside lid of the box of playing cards we noted what, at any rate to us, were outstanding scores. Recently I found this box in the cupboard where we kept the toys. The last date recorded was 9th March 1993, and I was pleased to note that on this occasion in a game with Christopher I had managed to achieve a double bezique. So my bezique playing had at least finished on a high note.

From time to time Winchester College honours some of its distinguished old boys by formally greeting them at the school 'ad portas' in Chamber Court, with the whole school and guests standing around the four sides of the court. In May 1981, while John was prefect of hall, the school honoured nine senior judges in this way. They wore their colourful robes, with the two members of the House of Lords in morning dress. John addressed them in Latin faultlessly and without a note. Lord Wilberforce, the senior judge and before whom I had appeared as counsel in the House of Lords, started his reply by adapting a phrase from the Odes of Horace: '*O matre pulchra filia pulchrior*'. He said: '*Exime praefecte aulae, patris facundi fili facundior…*' (distinguished prefect of hall, of an eloquent father the still more eloquent son).

For Jenny and me this was a day of immense pride.

From Winchester John obtained a scholarship in law at Trinity Hall, with a first in both parts of the Law Tripos and, just as important in his eyes, a (half) blue in football together with the captaincy of the Falcons (the university second team). In short, during the Cambridge terms he worked hard at his football and during the vacations when he was at home he worked hard at his law.

He was called to the Bar, as mentioned earlier, and went into practice in my old chambers, 13 Old Square, still playing football. Terence Cullen QC remarked jovially, 'A goalkeeper is just what we need in chambers.' In 1991 he married Divya Bhatia, another lawyer. She had graduated in law at St Edmund Hall, Oxford, and was practising in family law in the Temple. Following the precedent set by Jenny and me, they had met as bar students at the Middle Temple. They were married in St Bride's church, Fleet Street, by Canon Oates, with a reception afterwards in the hall of their Inn.

John greeting Lord Wilberforce 'ad portas'.

Finding a suitable school for Gill was more difficult. We decided she was probably not best suited for a boarding school. This left us with little choice, as the neighbourhood was not well endowed with girls' day schools. The Lady Eleanor Holles School, Hampton, seemed the best bet. Unfortunately, through no fault of hers, she never really settled there.

She had a difficult start. The school had a high reputation, and there was much demand for places. The surest way of obtaining entry to the senior school was to start in the junior school. This was not very satisfactory for it meant that, aged seven, she had a long day, leaving home on the school coach before 8am. Returning home on the coach in the afternoon meant she had to wait at school until the senior girls finished their longer day. When she returned home after 5pm she was tired. Homework had still to be done because, strangely, she was not allowed to do this at school while waiting for the coach.

Gill and Stephen, by the River Mole.

We kept hoping things would improve as she became older and more senior. There was a little improvement but, despite its high reputation, the school had some disappointing features at that time. The primary problem was that there was an almost total lack of pastoral care. When we wanted to discuss problems with the school staff we were not permitted to see Gill's form mistress. We had to see the headmistress. As she did not know Gill from Adam, as the saying goes, communication was manifestly hopeless. Nor were we ever permitted to see Gill's marked written work: 'The teachers would not like it,' we were told. I always felt the unspoken reason was concern by the teachers that parents might be critical of some of their marking. So we could not give Gill any of the help she so desperately needed.

At the top of the school Gill captained the school badminton team and played in the lacrosse team. But by then it had become apparent to us that her A level results would not do her justice. When Jenny raised the question of universities with the headmistress she dismissed this out of hand, suggesting a domestic science course. She did not countenance any question of Gill resitting her A levels.

When the results were announced our fears proved well founded, but we had already made arrangements for her to spend a year at a 'crammers' college (Davies's) in London after she left school. Impressively, she persevered at this and did well in her 'resits'. She was offered a place at Exeter University to read law. After graduating she qualified as a solicitor, practising with a firm based in Guildford.

In 1990 she married Stephen Christie, a fellow graduate from Exeter. He read computer science, and later business administration for an MBA at Heriot-Watt University, Edinburgh. In 2000 he was awarded a PhD by Surrey University. His thesis was *The management of market risk: regulation versus practice*. They were married in St Mary's church by the then rector, the Rev David Vincent, with a reception in a marquee in the garden at home.

Christopher followed in the footsteps of his brother and played in the same footballing position but headed towards a different goal. On one occasion in Cambridge I watched them playing on opposite sides in the same match. At Danes Hill he was a scholar and head of his house, then Winchester where he was an exhibitioner, school prefect and head of Morshead's house and, finally, at Trinity Hall where he chose to read economics. Perhaps over the years he had been served up too much law at home with Sunday lunch.

Christopher was attracted to a career in corporate finance, and qualified as a chartered accountant with Arthur Andersen, where he was an early pioneer of their 'scholarship programme'. Over the next twenty years he pursued his career with a most fortunate sense of timing: he left Arthur Andersen, before it went bust, to join Morgan Grenfell, now integrated within Deutsche Bank, then onto Lehman Brothers which he left before it, too, went bust, to join JPMorgan Cazenove. He is now a partner at Deloitte.

However busy, I always found time on Sunday evenings to write to each of the children away at school or university. In one year all three were away and one Sunday evening I decided, as a bit of fun, to send a letter with a difference. I wrote a 'round robin' containing a series of different greetings or wishes appropriate to one or more of the children. I then sent the same script to all three, but marking the particular passages appropriate to the recipient child. I never repeated this exercise. It took much longer to prepare than three separate letters.

In 2003 Christopher married Serena Hebeler whom he had met playing tennis. She was a graduate of Durham University, having read politics. Christopher had acquired a thatched cottage in the tranquil village of Great Tew in the Cotswolds,

Oxfordshire. They were married there by the rector Abbott Conway in the village church of St Michael and All Angels, a building listed grade I even though it had a hole in the roof. The church was packed, and as nearly everyone took communion the service was quite lengthy. So, to save time, Abbott omitted the hymn *Jerusalem* from the service. The service was followed, on the evening of a very hot sunny June day, by a magical reception in a marquee on the village cricket field.

At this reception, not to be done out of *Jerusalem*, after supper this hymn was sung with vigour by the guests. The only surprise was that all the young people knew the words by heart. One of the guests Janice Rich, wife of judge Michael Rich QC, later wrote to us:

'The setting was idyllic and I can see why they are both so enamoured by that patch of England. When we stood and sang *Jerusalem* looking out of the tent over 'a green and pleasant land' it was just one of the many moments that brought a lump to one's throat.'

CHAPTER 20

Change Of Venue
House of Lords: October 1994

IN THE SUMMER of 1994 I was invited to become, to use the formal title, a lord of appeal in ordinary. In short, a full time judge who is a peer.

Historically, in addition to its legislative function, the House of Lords had a judicial function, but the jurisdiction of professionally qualified lords of appeal was a statutory creation of the 1870s. 'Ordinary' indicated that these judges had a particular jurisdiction, exercised by virtue of their office. Unlike other peers they were paid a salary. They heard appeals from the courts of appeal of England, Wales and Northern Ireland and in civil cases from the Scottish High Court of Justiciary and Court of Session. Known colloquially as 'law lords', they were the court of final appeal in the United Kingdom. In 2009 this jurisdiction was replaced by the newly created Supreme Court of the United Kingdom.

Over the years the number of lords of appeal gradually increased to twelve. They normally sat in groups of five, although occasionally seven or even nine. They comprised nine judges from England and Wales, two judges from Scotland and one from Northern Ireland. Usually the English judges had held office as lords justices in the Court of Appeal but not always. Exceptionally Lord Wilberforce was promoted straight from the High Court and, some years earlier, Lord Radcliffe was appointed directly from the Bar as, more recently, was Lord Sumption to the Supreme Court. One of the Scottish judges had usually held office in Scotland as lord president of the Court of Session and the Irish judge as lord chief justice of Northern Ireland.

One important factor in the choice of the English judges was the need to ensure, as far as possible, that between them the law lords had expertise in the fields of work most often coming before them. This changes from time to time. In the 1950s and 1960s a substantial proportion of the appeals were tax cases. This volume fell to a trickle by the end of the century, and was replaced by judicial review and human rights appeals.

Before the second world war lords of appeal heard appeals in the magnificent chamber of the House of Lords, as part of the business of the House. They sat as the House of Lords. Usually, but by no means always, the lord chancellor presided

Being sworn in the House of Lords with supporters
Lord Woolf and Lord Chief Justice Taylor.

at these judicial sessions. Procedurally these sittings were essentially the same as for other business, with the mace on the woolsack, representing royal authority, and a bishop reading prayers at the outset of the session. Apart from the nature of the business the only other difference was that, although 'lay' peers could attend the judicial sittings, they could not take part in them.

The exclusion of lay peers in this way had not always been so. When the Duke of Buccleuch was lord president of the council in the 1840s he was asked to sit on an appeal from India. He hesitated because he was not qualified to sit and hear the case. 'Don't worry, your grace,' he was told, 'the natives in India would much prefer their case to be decided by a great Scottish duke than by a common lawyer.'

The judicial sessions were always heard at the outset of the day's business, usually 10.30am and continuing to 4pm, and the peers sat for their regular business at 4.30pm.

During the war the Commons chamber was bombed, in 1941. The Commons moved to the Lords chamber, and the Lords conducted their business in the royal robing room at the southern end of the palace. After the war the noise of rebuilding works made conditions in that room intolerable during the day. In 1948, purely as a temporary measure, an appellate committee was appointed to enable the law lords to hear appeals without disturbance in one of the committee rooms on the first floor. The judgments of the law lords continued to be given in the chamber. Unlike other senior judges, the law lords sat unrobed, whether in the chamber or as a committee, that being the dress of other peers when conducting business. Counsel were robed, in both places.

As often happens, a temporary expedient became a permanent fixture. After the reason for their migration had gone the law lords continued to hear appeals in a committee room sitting as the appellate committee of the House. All that remained of the original arrangements was that from time to time one or two appeals were heard in the chamber when the House was not sitting, the law lords thereby underlining their status as members of the House.

Having heard appeals in both venues I have to say that, undoubtedly, the layout of the committee room was much better suited for hearing appeals than the chamber. This is hardly surprising. The chamber was not constructed as a courtroom. It was built in the 19th century as a grand debating chamber, complete with a throne for the monarch.

One consequence of the appellate committee becoming a fixture, as was apparent by the early 1950s, was that the House advanced its time of sitting from 4.30pm to 2.30pm. The lord chancellor was expected to take his seat on the woolsack at the beginning of each day's business, so it became more difficult for him to sit judicially.

Gradually and progressively lord chancellors presided less and less over appeals to the House. This was for a combination of reasons: the timetable of government business – the lord chancellor was a member of the cabinet – the expansion of the work of the lord chancellor's office, and the emergence of the principle that the lord chancellor should not sit on public law cases. Increasingly lord chancellors became less involved in matters expected of heads of divisions, such as selecting the panels of law lords to sit on future cases. By the early 1980s the meetings to decide these matters took place in the law lords' conference room between the two senior law lords, the clerk of the judicial office and the registrar of the Privy Council. The term 'senior law lord' was increasingly used to describe the law lord who, in practice, had taken over much of the administrative work relating to the law lords previously done by the lord chancellor.

At first this term was not accepted universally. James Vallance White, clerk of the judicial office, recalls Lord Hailsham disliking it so much that, on hearing it, he was apt to greet the speaker with the expostulation: 'Kindly remember that *I* am the senior law lord.' The first formal appointment of a senior law lord was in 2000 when Lord Bingham of Cornhill was appointed to that office direct from his post as lord chief justice. I was appointed second senior lord of appeal by letters patent on 1st October 2002, although not by that name. The offices of senior and second senior lord of appeal in ordinary were first recognised in legislation in the Constitutional Reform Act 2005. Ironically, that recognition was for the purpose of abolishing those offices on the creation of the new Supreme Court.

In my day judgments were given in the chamber at 9.45am. These brief sittings followed the usual procedures of the House: dead on time, a retired sergeant major marched into the chamber with the mace on his shoulder and laid it on the woolsack with military aplomb, and a bishop then read the prayers. Judgments, with counsel attending silently at the bar of the House, lasted about fifteen or twenty minutes, and the House then adjourned until the commencement of its ordinary business, normally in the afternoon. The judgments took the form of individual speeches, followed immediately by votes cast on formal questions. At one time the speeches, however long, were read out in full, but in my time individual lords of appeal merely stated their conclusions, for instance, 'The appeal should be dismissed for the reasons I have set out in print'. On these occasions the senior or the second senior lord of appeal sat on the woolsack and put the formal questions. I cannot recall the lord chancellor ever doing so in my twelve years as a law lord.

Committee room one, where the appellate committee invariably sat, was an oblong room on the first floor at one end of a long corridor of committee rooms. It was a quietly beautiful room, with a very different atmosphere from an ordinary law court. It had a fascinating view over the river through large windows, with huge portraits of distinguished peers hung against heavily papered walls. The law lords sat on one side of the room behind an extensive horseshoe-shaped bench at the same level as the parties.

As with any law court in this country, members of the public were entitled to admission, but few came. The general public seem not to have appreciated that, tucked away inside the Houses of Parliament, was this country's court of final appeal. Certainly the security arrangements confronting those seeking to enter the palace were a little daunting.

The appellate committee followed the same procedures as other committees of the House. Unlike in courts of law, the lawyers and the parties were kept waiting outside in the corridor until the lords of appeal were seated. At the end of the hearing the presiding law lord announced that 'their lordships will report their decision to the House in due course.' The usher then called 'clear the bar', meaning the bar beyond which the lawyers and parties had been sitting, and bustled everybody out of the room, locking the door behind them and leaving the law lords by themselves. One by one, starting with the most junior, each expressed his or her view on the outcome of the appeal. This usually took about half an hour, sometimes much longer. At this stage we decided who would write the first judgment.

In most cases bringing an appeal before the House of Lords required permission from the law lords themselves. Sometimes, but infrequently, permission to appeal was given by the Court of Appeal. Infrequently because, as Lord Bingham said on one occasion, 'their Lordships prefer to dine à la carte, choosing for themselves the matters they wish to digest.' When I was sitting in the Court of Appeal I gave permission only when it was self-evident that, if asked the law lords would grant permission and, very occasionally, when an existing decision of the law lords, which bound the Court of Appeal, plainly needed to be reviewed by the lords, whether they wished to do so or not.

The law lords had individual rooms on the second floor, mostly overlooking Westminster Abbey. We shared secretaries. When I visited the House before I took my seat one of the law lords advised me that the secretarial facilities were far from satisfactory and I should learn to type. So Jenny went to the Cobham public library and borrowed an ancient Pitman book on how to type. I slaved away during the long vacation in 1994 and became able to 'touch type' to a reasonable standard.

Before I was sworn in I had to pay a visit to the College of Arms for a meeting with 'Garter' (garter king of arms) to decide my title. Every peer has a distinctive title. Most peers use their existing surnames, but to achieve this distinctiveness while retaining his surname a peer often needs to add a territorial suffix. I had to do this because of the risk of confusion with Baroness Nicol. The peer must have some connection with the chosen place name as, for example, I have with Birkenhead.

I was introduced to the House of Lords on 19th October 1994. This was a full and happy family day. First, Jenny and the family had a pre-lunch drink with the lord chancellor in his room. Next, in accordance with tradition, I gave lunch in the House to several people connected with the occasion and some close friends. We had a party of fifteen. In addition to Jenny and our children and their spouses the guests, with their formal titles, were: Lord Mackay of Clashfern (lord high chancellor), Lord Taylor of Gosforth (lord chief justice), Lord and Lady Woolf, Sir Michael Wheeler-Booth (clerk of the parliaments), Sir Conrad Swan (garter principal king of arms) and the Very Reverend Dr Brandon Jackson (dean of Lincoln) and Mary Jackson.

Law lords in 1997: (standing), Lords Hope, Nicholls, Nolan, Hoffmann, Slynn, Steyn, Clyde, Hutton, (seated) Lords Lloyd, Browne-Wilkinson, Mackay (Lord Chancellor), Goff and Mustill.

Lord Taylor and Lord Woolf were my 'supporters'. Their function was to accompany me on either side when I was ushered into the chamber to take my oath.

After lunch I donned my peers' robes, as did my two supporters. We proceeded into the chamber with much bowing on all sides. The clerk read out my letters patent. In the case of lords of appeal the appointment is to hold office only 'so long as he shall well behave himself therein'. This proviso always causes a ripple of amusement from other peers in the chamber. Their appointments are not subject to this proviso.

I then swore an oath of allegiance, and shook hands with the lord chancellor who was sitting on the woolsack, whereupon all the peers murmured their approval. The other lords of appeal kindly attended for the occasion.

Having removed my robes I returned to the chamber and took my seat for the first time, as a cross-bencher, and listened to question time. Downstairs, waiting for me in the cloakroom, was a vast red box containing my letters patent sealed with the great seal. This is a seal used to symbolise the sovereign's approval of important state documents. It is about six inches in diameter, engraved with images of the Queen on each side.

To complete the day Brandon and Mary and the family all went off together to Brown's hotel, in central London, for tea. Divya had managed to persuade the hotel, contrary to its usual practice, to reserve seats for us all on this special occasion.

New peers are encouraged to make their first speech ('maiden speech') sooner rather than later. I made my maiden speech a few months later. One feature of procedure in the Lords is that eldest sons of peers are entitled to sit on the steps of the throne and listen to debates. John availed himself of this right. Christopher availed himself of his right to stand at the bar of the House. Jenny and Gaynor were also present, but they had seats.

The subject of the debate was conditional fees. For centuries conditional fees ('no win, no fee') were regarded as offending the ancient prohibition against champerty. Champerty was the support of court proceedings by a stranger in return for a share of the proceeds. But the drastic reduction of access to legal aid had left an increasing number of people stranded. The middle class were too rich to qualify for legal aid and often too poor to consider court proceedings. By reducing serious financial risk conditional fees were aimed at making justice more accessible.

In the debate I spoke in favour of a statutory instrument enabling the use of such fees in today's conditions. I said:

'My Lords, I am gratefully fortified by the kind remarks of my noble and learned Lord Ackner. It is still with considerable trepidation that I rise. I do so with two pieces of advice I received ringing in my ears. The first was that I should keep my speech short, advice that cannot be repeated too frequently for lawyers. The second piece of advice I received was that I should speak on a subject about which I care.

I care about the state of the law. I care that the legal system should, in practice as well as in jurisprudential theory, give a remedy to all who are legally wronged. I am concerned that financial might should not oust legal right.

For some years until recently I was the head of one of the three divisions of the High Court. That division, the Chancery Division, comprises seventeen High Court judges. They are all exceptionally able people, and they are all highly motivated. But, as vice-chancellor, I became ever more concerned about the sheer cost, the prohibitive expense, of bringing and conducting proceedings in front of those excellent people. I could not afford to be involved in proceedings in the High Court. Nor could most individuals who are not legally aided.

How does this situation come about? What has gone wrong? I suggest there can be only one answer to those questions. Although the law has developed as society has changed, the legal system still lags behind. The system contains many checks and balances, some excellent and some essential but some now operate as a brake on progress. Procedures and provisions that were necessary and valuable as safeguards in a less sophisticated and non-technical society now, I believe, in some instances, overall do more harm than good.

In those circumstances where do we go? I apprehend that everything I have said is now widely recognised. It is also widely recognised that there is no simple solution. There is no single solution. Before your Lordships' House this afternoon is a Question concerning one particular proposed item of reform of legal procedure. On this occasion I am subject to the restraint that I must not be provocative – as if I ever would be. So I confine myself to just one observation of a very generalised nature.

Proposals for the reform of the legal system arouse strong feelings on both sides. That leads to misunderstandings, which hamper rather than help. I venture to suggest to those who support reform that they should recognise that the strength of feelings of those who oppose particular reforms is no more than a measure of the depth of their concern that the legal system should function properly. They are concerned that well intentioned proposals for reform should not damage but, rather, improve. Conversely, I venture to suggest to those who oppose particular reforms that they should recognise that to every proposal for a reform of the legal system some objection can be raised. I apprehend there is no proposed reform that could be made without some risk. If we wait for a proposal which will be universally welcomed, to which there are no appendant risks and which has no possible ground for objection, we shall wait for reform truly for ever.

In those circumstances, of course, reforms must be thought through. Of course there must be consultation, of course we must all have the humility to learn from the experience of other countries. But there must come a time in the process – I do not allude indirectly to the matter your Lordships are considering this afternoon – when a proposal which on its face would improve access to justice should be favourably received unless there are truly compelling reasons why that should not be so. Only if some such approach is adopted will we, sooner rather than later, bring about necessary changes for the advantage of those for whom the legal system exists at all.'.

Some law lords and other peers were strongly opposed to the introduction of conditional fees. Next day The Times urged Lord Mackay to resist pressure to dilute his reforms. The Times leader continued: 'As Lord Nicholls of Birkenhead said in his polished maiden speech in the House of Lords, a proposal that "would improve access to justice should be favourably received unless there are truly compelling reasons why that should not be so."'

In due course conditional fee legislation came into operation although not, I must say, without teething problems.

The Queen's Council
Judicial Committee: October 1994

IN MY DAY, although not widely realised in the legal profession, the law lords spent as much of their time sitting on the judicial committee of the Privy Council as in the House of Lords.

This committee was established by statute early in the 19th century to hear appeals previously heard by the King-in-Council. At that time the jurisdiction of the Privy Council was extremely wide. The council heard appeals from all parts of the old British Empire, which comprised countries having a substantial proportion of the population of the world: the Indian subcontinent, Canada, South Africa, Rhodesia, Malaya, Singapore, Hong Kong, Australia, New Zealand and many other countries.

One by one in the 20th century most of these countries shouldered responsibility for their own final courts of appeal. In my time the principal customers of the judicial committee were New Zealand, Jamaica, Trinidad and Tobago, and Hong Kong. Hong Kong set up its own Court of Final Appeal in 1997 and New Zealand in 2003.

The formal procedure was that, in most instances, the appeals were made to Her Majesty in council, who then referred the case to the judicial committee for 'advice'. The committee's judgment took the form of a 'report' to the Queen in council.

For many years the judicial committee sat in the spacious and historic Privy Council chamber in Downing Street. A stately limousine, into which five law lords could squeeze with varying degrees of discomfort, was set aside for transporting them from the 'House' to the 'Privy'. In my day the car was temperamental and at times reluctant to start. Then, or when the weather was fine, we walked the short distance to or fro. I was less disposed to walk to Downing Street after security was tightened and, like everyone else, we were searched at the gates. This search did not take place when we were riding in our 'limo' because this vehicle was well recognised as 'the judges' car'. Occasionally there were public demonstrations in Whitehall outside the gates, and then we could escape the crowds on our return to the House of Lords by taking a circuitous route on foot through the Foreign Office building on the other side of Downing Street.

Like the car, the court room was something of a period piece. It was not well adapted to modern requirements. It was cold in winter and hot in summer. But it was highly atmospheric as the very place from which in a bygone age justice had been administered to such a large part of the world.

From October 2009 the sittings of the committee were moved to one of the courts in the old Middlesex Guildhall building which now houses the Supreme Court of the United Kingdom.

Judges in the Court of Appeal were eligible to sit on the judicial committee because they were privy councillors. They did so, infrequently, whenever there were not enough law lords available. Occasionally so did retired law lords. For instance, Lord Griffiths, formerly a law lord, sat for a while after he had retired when I was newly appointed to the Lords. He was a man of many parts: much in demand at all levels in the legal world, he excelled also as a cricketer and golfer, awarded a Cambridge blue in both fields, played county cricket for Glamorgan, and later became president of the MCC and captain of the Royal and Ancient at St Andrews.

Likewise in some years one of the New Zealand Court of Appeal judges, including Sean Elias, the chief justice, came over to London and joined us on sittings of the judicial committee. They were all excellent lawyers and delightful people. It was a joy to sit with them, as it was with Robin Cooke, a former president of the New Zealand Court of Appeal. He was outstandingly able and for some years spent several months in England each year.

Some of the New Zealand judges were very keen on rugby. Their visits to England were timed to coincide with international rugby matches at Twickenham. Once, to his amusement, I ribbed a New Zealand judge by telling him he would have to sit with Johan Steyn and Lenny Hoffmann, both from South Africa, even though this meant there would not be a level playing field.

On these visits by New Zealand judges I was embarrassed we were not able to be more hospitable. The difficulty, as always, was pressure of work. It was one thing to escort them to lunch in the House of Lords but, alas, to entertain them in the evening or at the weekend when we were out of London was much more difficult.

Overall, I have to say, I did not greatly enjoy my work on the judicial committee. I disliked the waste of time in getting to and from Downing Street in the morning and again in the afternoon. More importantly, a significant part of the work involved hearing capital cases, that is, appeals in murder cases where the mandatory punishment was death. In these cases London barristers and city solicitors acted on behalf of the accused and provided their services pro bono (free). The outcome of these appeals usually depended on a thorough analysis of the conduct of the trial, including the judge's summing up. Some of the law lords were highly experienced in this field but I was not. I was never wholly comfortable.

CHAPTER 22

Not Always A Judge
Other Commitments: 1996

IF FIVE LAW lords were sitting each day in the House of Lords and another five in the 'Privy' that would suggest that at any time two law lords were free to get on with writing judgments. This was not so. The number of law lords was increased from ten to twelve precisely because of other demands on the law lords' time. The most notable instance was the 'Bloody Sunday' inquiry tribunal chaired by Lord Saville of Newdigate, full time, for over ten years, from 1998 to 2010. Lord Nolan was the first chairman of the committee on standards in public life from 1992 to 1996.

For my sins I was chairman of the lord chancellor's advisory committee on legal education and conduct, for two years from 1996 to 1997. This committee was set up in 1991 as an independent body, part of new machinery established by statute to oversee the provision of legal services in England and Wales. The members were a mixture of lawyers and non-lawyers, with non-lawyers in the majority.

In practice the principal function of the committee was to give advice to the lord chancellor on legal education and continuing legal education and on the grant of rights of audience and rights to conduct litigation. The committee met every fortnight, with additional meetings for sub-committees.

I found my work as chairman very time-consuming. This played havoc with my participation in hearing appeals in the House of Lords. So I was pleased when Lord Irvine of Lairg, who had succeeded Lord Mackay as lord chancellor, asked me to chair a committee on parliamentary privilege. This gave me the opportunity to be relieved from the chairmanship of the advisory committee. I could not do both jobs satisfactorily at the same time. As it turned out, this new commitment occupied me fully for about eighteen months.

The background to this committee was that in June 1997 ministers in both Houses of Parliament announced that, as part of an initiative to modernise Parliament, the government proposed to institute a general review of parliamentary privilege. The joint committee was set up on 30th July. The committee included representatives from the three major parties in each House. Apart from me they were all experienced parliamentarians. Happily, some of them were also experienced lawyers: Lord Mayhew of Twysden, formerly attorney general, Lord Wigoder, Lord Waddington GCVO, and Lord Archer of Sandwell (formerly solicitor general). I was elected chairman at the first meeting of the committee in October.

The committee placed advertisements in four national newspapers and received over 150 letters and memoranda. It held fourteen sessions of evidence in public and altogether thirty-three meetings.

This was a fascinating exercise, with interesting evidence from many distinguished people. Parliamentary privilege covers a wide range of subjects, such as freedom of speech in Parliament, control by Parliament of its own affairs, and disciplinary and penal powers. In reviewing this field the committee applied the touchstone that Parliament should be vigilant to retain necessary rights and immunities and equally rigorous in discarding all others. It is not surprising that at times these criteria generated differing views within the committee. We had some lively discussions.

The committee's unanimous report was finalised in February 1999 and laid before each House on 30th March 1999. The report made thirty-nine recommendations. With two qualifications the government accepted the report in debate in the House of Commons. There was no debate in the House of Lords.

CHAPTER 23

China
Hong Kong Court of Final Appeal: 1999

MY INVOLVEMENT WITH Hong Kong was of an altogether different character. On my visits there I sat as a judge of Hong Kong's Court of Final Appeal. That was a remarkable experience, acting as a judge of another country's most senior court.

Hong Kong was established as a colony of the British Empire after the first opium war in 1841. Later it became a British dependent territory. On 1st July 1997 sovereignty was transferred to China. Hong Kong became the first Special Administrative Region of the Peoples' Republic of China, on the principle of 'one country, two systems'. The 'basic law', the territory's constitutional document, enshrined the independence of the judiciary and the continuation of English common law. Judges from common law countries could be recruited to serve as non-permanent judges.

Initially six overseas judges were recruited, two from Australia, two from New Zealand, and two from England: Lord Hoffmann and myself. The overseas judges never sat together. The procedure was that one of the six sat with the chief justice, Andrew Li, and the three permanent members of the Court of Final Appeal. The overseas judges took turns in their visits to Hong Kong at times which suited them and when there were appeals calling for decision.

As might be expected we had to take a judicial oath. Initially this caused some difficulty, because the oath included an oath of allegiance: '… I will bear allegiance to the Hong Kong Special Administrative Region of the Peoples' Republic of China.' In the course of my judicial career I must have sworn allegiance to the Queen on upwards of a dozen occasions. At first blush to swear allegiance to another country seemed inconsistent. Eventually it was all sorted out, after consultation at the 'highest level', on the basis that the Hong Kong oath applied only to work done by us as judges of the Hong Kong Court of Final Appeal.

I was appointed as a non-permanent judge for two tranches of three years, starting in January 1998. Jenny and I went to Hong Kong twice, once for four weeks and once for three weeks. On the second of these visits Christopher and Serena called in on their way to holidaying in Bali and joined us for lunch with Andrew Li and his wife Judy.

Hong Kong was a marvellous place to visit. It has some exceptional features: a deep natural harbour; the world's most vertical city; a highly developed transport network with the public transport travelling rate exceeding 90%, the highest in the world; the third most important international financial centre after New York and London. As much of Hong Kong's terrain is hilly or mountainous only one quarter of its landmass is developed. Despite this it is one of the most densely populated areas in the world.

On our visits we were warmly welcomed on all sides. At times too much so, I have to say at the risk of sounding ungrateful. I had a busy work schedule and coping with evening functions and making speeches on top of this was quite wearing. The dinners included a Trinity Hall law reunion, attended by John Collier, a law don who had taught John law and football, and a reunion of some Liverpool University graduates.

We stayed in a splendid hotel, the Conrad, on a high floor (I think it was the fifty-first). The hotel was within easy walking distance of the court. The court building had originally been the French mission, close by St John's cathedral. These were two of the few small buildings surviving in the central district. Otherwise the buildings were modern office blocks, all reaching for the sky.

'Vertical living' was not altogether to our taste. A snag with vertical living on the Hong Kong scale was a shortage of sunshine out of doors. The skyscraper buildings cast long shadows, and it was not easy to find somewhere to sit in the sun in central Hong Kong. Additionally at times the air was heavily polluted. On one morning the pollution blown across from the mainland during the night was so dense that until the hotel windows were cleaned it was impossible to see through them.

We did some sightseeing at the weekends. If it was a Sunday we had to pick our way through the throngs of chattering Filipino girls busily doing each other's hair. We visited the zoo. We chugged across Victoria harbour to Kowloon on one of the green-and-white Star ferries. We rode on the funicular tramway up the Peak and walked round its perimeter for about an hour. We took a bus to Stanley village, where Paul Chanin, Stephen's 'best man', and his wife Clare were living with their children in a delightful house.

Most mornings Jenny walked across Victoria Park and through the ground floor of several buildings to a sandwich shop where she bought herself some lunch. My lunch sandwich came from the same shop so she thought it must be OK. One morning she was bold and sought to get some money from a hole-in-the-wall

Hong Kong, with the Chief Minister and Chief Justice Li.

machine. Unfortunately she put her card into the wrong slot. This set off alarm bells, closed down the machine and brought out the guards, not to mention the spectators. She managed to recover her card with the help of the bank manager, but in future money collection was left to me.

One of the permanent judges of the Court of Final Appeal, Kemy Bokhary, and his wife Verina, herself a High Court judge, were particularly kind to us. He is an outstanding judge, with strong views about democratic government and the need for the law to keep abreast of the times. It was always a joy to work with him, and to see them both on their trips to London where they had a flat used by their three delightful daughters.

On our second visit to Hong Kong I had an opportunity to assist in bringing the Hong Kong Court of Final Appeal into the international legal limelight. Freedom of speech is a highly sensitive subject in Hong Kong and the case concerned defamation.

The law of defamation is complex. It provides a number of defences to a claim based on a defamatory statement. One of these is fair comment or, more accurately, honest comment. To satisfy this defence the comment must satisfy several ingredients. Loosely stated, these are that the comment must be on a matter of public interest; it must be recognisable as comment as distinct from an imputation of fact; it must be based on true facts, and it must be a comment an honest person could make. Even if a defendant satisfies these conditions he may still be liable if the plaintiff proves that when the defendant made his comment he was actuated by 'malice'.

But what does this time-honoured expression mean in this context? Having considered all the cases and the practical implications I concluded that a defendant who satisfies each of the ingredients mentioned above will lose his immunity only by proof that he did not genuinely hold the view he expressed. Honesty of belief is the touchstone. Actuation by motives such as spite, animosity, intent to injure or to arouse controversy does not of itself defeat the defence, but proof of such motivation may be evidence from which lack of genuine belief may be inferred.

This approach, agreed by all the members of the court, represented a marked departure from the view generally expressed hitherto. So far as I know this analysis was accepted throughout the common law world. In the textbooks the authority cited in support was this decision of the Hong Kong Court of Final Appeal. In England and Wales the Defamation Act 2013 has now replaced the defence of 'fair comment' with a defence of 'honest opinion'.

CHAPTER 24

Time To Change
Keeping The Law up to Date

ONE MAJOR FUNCTION of a court of last resort is correcting errors which have crept into the common law ('judge-made law') or into the interpretation of statutes. The Hong Kong appeal just mentioned is an instance. Another function, of vital importance, is updating the common law in appropriate cases in response to the increasing sophistication of society.

Law is the set of rules by which society is ordered. Common law principles are intended to achieve a just result or, as I prefer to say in this context, maintain a fair balance between competing interests. That is their fundamental objective. Certainty is important. People need to know how to regulate their conduct and affairs, but this is not an overriding consideration. Social conditions are not immutable. If a legal principle no longer strikes a fair balance there is something wrong. Most frequently, this occurs when expectations of what is fair and reasonable, 'the spirit of the times', have changed. A law acceptable in one century, or even in one decade, may not be acceptable in the next. Then the law no longer achieves its fundamental objective. When administering the law judges must recognise this and respond accordingly. The law must keep abreast of the times in which we live, otherwise it falls into disrepute as unrealistic and out of date.

To this end, and this is peculiarly the function of courts of final appeal, judges need to identify relevant changes in social conditions. Sometimes there is overt pressure for a change in the law by 'pressure groups' on a highly controversial subject. Then the way forward is not clear because there are differing views. That is not a circumstance calling for intervention by the judges. If there is to be a change in the law, Parliament must so decide. Euthanasia is a good example.

In other cases the starting point, very often, is when a legal proposition evokes an immediate response of 'that cannot be right; that cannot be the state of the law today.' Then the judges have to weigh all the pros and cons and 'develop' the law incrementally and appropriately if, but only if, the need for change is plain and compelling. Notably in the 1970s and 1980s judges developed the scope of judicial review as a remedy for the abuse of ever-increasing national and local governmental powers. Perhaps the best known example of a single court decision changing the law is the case concerning the decomposed remains of a snail said to be in a bottle of ginger beer. In 1932, in *Donoghue v Stevenson*, the House of Lords changed the common law by deciding that a manufacturer owes a duty of care to the ultimate consumer of goods he puts into circulation.

In order to give some idea of this aspect of my work as a lord of appeal I set out below three recent examples of judges bringing the law up to date by recognising the time had come for change. These are instances of development in the common law, the application of statute law to a novel situation, and changing the way judges exercise a statutory discretion.

As I have said, it is not always possible for the judges to keep the law up to date in this way. A change may plainly be needed but this may be a matter for Parliament and not the judges. I illustrate this with a criminal law appeal, heard unusually by the judicial committee sitting as an enlarged board of nine law lords.

My first example had international ramifications. It concerned Senator Augusto Pinochet, formerly the president of Chile. In November 1998 Senator Pinochet was in England having medical treatment. The government of Spain sought to extradite him to Spain to stand trial there in respect of serious crimes, genocide, murder on a large scale, torture and hostage-taking, for which he was said to have been responsible in Chile when he was head of state. The sole question before the House was whether, by reason of his status as a former head of state, he was immune from the criminal processes of this country. Extradition forms part of these processes.

The legal issues are too complicated to summarise. Never was I more mindful that the House of Lords is a court of last resort. Suffice to say, by a majority of three to two, the House answered this question in the negative: Pinochet was not immune. This was a departure from the more traditional view. The majority were Lord Steyn, Lord Hoffmann and myself.

The case attracted much attention, national and international. When the House was delivering its short summary opinions in the chamber there were noisy crowds outside. As soon as the result was announced we could hear the prolonged cheering.

For the one and only time, so far as I know, my face appeared in *Le Monde*, inaccurately showing me wearing a wig, over the text: 'Lord Nicholls of Birkenhead est l'un des trois magistrats suprêmes britanniques à avoir opiné – avec succès – contre le maintien de l'immunité de l'ancien chef d'Etat chilien.' *Le Monde* said the ruling was 'English genius' which marked the moment 'when fear changed sides'. *France-Soir* said the lords had never so justly deserved to be called noble.

Elation, of course, was not universal. General Pinochet's supporters were dismayed. The headline in *The Guardian* was: 'From London to Santiago the verdict on Pinochet brings anger and joy.'

This was not the end of the story. One of the parties permitted to intervene in the appeal and make submissions was Amnesty International. Lord Hoffmann was an unpaid director of the charitable arm of that organisation. When this came to light, a differently constituted panel of five law lords set aside the previous decision. Lord Hoffmann should have been disqualified from sitting on the basis of apparent bias. A third panel, again differently constituted, heard the appeal anew.

At this rehearing the overall outcome was much the same as it was first time round. I was not surprised, because I felt that the decision of Johan Steyn, Lenny Hoffmann and me had 'broken the mould'. We had set the law on a new course, even though our decision was set aside on the ground that Lenny should have recused (disqualified) himself.

In the end Senator Pinochet was not extradited. Because of his ill health Jack Straw, secretary of state for the home office, declined to make an extradition order.

One effect of this unhappy sequence of three hearings in the House of Lords was that this encouraged parties' solicitors in future, in advance of a hearing, to search through all the public records, for instance, of lectures, to see if any law lord had ever expressed views contrary to their client's interests on the legal issues involved in the current case. If yes, they used this as a means of objecting to a particular law lord. As happened in at least one later appeal.

Increasingly, in appeals raising important issues of legal principle, the law lords were permitting intervention by outside parties when they had something to contribute. We were concerned that the submissions should be presented fully. Like many other judges I was a member of JUSTICE, an all-party law reform and human rights organisation. So I promptly resigned, in order to prevent my continuing membership of that organisation precluding me from hearing cases in which JUSTICE was permitted to intervene.

My second example concerns an everyday problem: the division of property when a marriage ends in divorce. The decision in the case of Mr and Mrs White in October 2000 heralded a radical change in the judicial approach to the exercise of the statutory powers to make financial provision orders when granting a decree of divorce.

Typically, more in the past than today, the husband went out and earned the money and the wife looked after the home. In a 'clean break' case where the available assets exceeded the parties' financial needs (so-called 'big money' cases) the practice was to regard the wife's 'reasonable requirements' as a determinative and limiting factor on the amount of her award.

Social attitudes have changed. Everyone accepts that the division of assets should be fair. Today there is greater awareness of the value of non-financial contributions to the welfare of the family. In seeking to achieve a fair outcome, there is no place for discrimination between husband and wife and their respective roles. There should be no bias in favour of the money-earner and against the home-maker and the child-carer. I said:

> 'The traditional division of labour is no longer the order of the day. Frequently both parents work. Sometimes it is the wife who is the money-earner and the husband runs the home and cares for the children during the day. But whatever the division of labour chosen by the husband and wife, or forced upon them by circumstances, fairness requires that this should not prejudice or advantage either party … As a general guide, equality should be departed from only if, and to the extent that, there is good reason for doing so.'

I posed the rhetorical questions:

> 'If a husband and wife by their joint efforts over many years, his directly in his business and hers indirectly at home, have built up a valuable business from scratch, why should the claimant wife be confined to the court's assessment of her reasonable requirements and the husband left with a much larger share? Or, to put the question differently, in such a case, where the assets exceed the financial needs of both parties, why should the surplus belong solely to the husband?'

The Independent newspaper described this as a 'ground-breaking judgment' and the *Financial Times* as a 'revolution' in the divorce laws. *The Guardian* said the judgment 'acknowledges that the family courts have failed to keep pace with the times.'

Six years later the House of Lords revisited this area of law, in the cases of Miller and McFarlane. The speeches were lengthy and complex. I mention only one point, in an abbreviated form. In order to achieve consistency and predictability in this field I sought to give guidance, in principle, on the requirements of fairness. The primary requirement is making provision for the welfare of the children of the marriage. Beyond this there are three requirements: financial needs, compensation (redressing any prospective economic disparity arising from the way the parties conducted their marriage), and sharing (when the marriage partnership ends each is entitled to an equal share of the partnership assets unless there is good reason to the contrary). Baroness Hale's speech was to much the same effect although we differed on one point.

The Times commented that this was the most important divorce judgment for twenty years, with a ruling which brings some clarity to a chaotic system. *The Sunday Times* said the ruling was 'one of the most important decisions about British divorce ever made … which has already become a towering landmark in our long and colourful divorce history.' The article continued:

> 'With his House of Lords ruling, Nicholls has changed the face of divorce. But he has done so by rearranging existing statute and precedent, bringing them more in line with contemporary reality and notions of fairness.
>
> The foundation of his reasoning was …'Fairness is an elusive concept. It is an instinctive response to a given set of facts. Ultimately it is grounded in social and moral values … they change from one generation to the next.'
>
> In other words, it is not the job of the law to define fairness but to reflect contemporary attitudes. It is this fundamental statement that turns the ruling into a key document of British social history.'

I turn next to a different type of case, concerning Martin Fitzpatrick, where the courts had to formulate the law's response to a novel question. For many years successive Rent Acts afforded residential tenants the benefit of fair rentals and protection from eviction. The protection extended to the original tenant and members of his 'family'. The statutes did not define 'family'. The law has long recognised that an unmarried man and woman living together without children could constitute 'family'. That was a decision of Lord Denning sitting as master of the rolls in the Court of Appeal in 1975. The novel question raised before the House of Lords in 1999 was whether two men or two women living together could constitute 'family'.

The judges were divided. The Court of Appeal, by a majority of two to one, said 'no'. The House of Lords, again by a bare majority of three to two, decided 'yes'. I was one of the majority. My reasoning was straightforward:

> 'A man and woman living together in a stable and permanent sexual relationship are capable of being members of a family for this purpose. Once this is accepted, there can be no rational or other basis on which the like conclusion can be withheld from a similarly stable and permanent sexual relationship between two men or between two women. Where a relationship of this character exists, it cannot make sense to say that, although a heterosexual partnership can give rise to membership of a family for Rent Act purposes, a

homosexual partnership cannot. Where sexual partners are involved, whether heterosexual or homosexual, there is scope for the intimate mutual love and affection and long-term commitment that typically characterise the relationship of husband and wife. This love and affection and commitment can exist in same sex relationships as in heterosexual relationships. In sexual terms a homosexual relationship is different from a heterosexual relationship, but I am unable to see that the difference is material for present purposes. … the concept underlying membership of a family for present purposes is the sharing of lives together in a single family unit living in one house.'

Lord Slynn of Hadley reached the same conclusion, saying this was 'in accordance with contemporary notions of social justice'.

The press gave considerable publicity to this decision without comment either way: 'Judges give homosexuals new legal status', 'Homosexual tenants win "family" rights', 'Lords' gay ruling redefines the family', and 'Gays have same rights as married couples say Lords.'

My final example from the House of Lords concerns another legal issue of huge practical importance: the interaction between freedom of speech and protection of reputation. The context was a newspaper discussion of a matter of political importance. During the political crisis in Dublin in November 1994 Mr Reynolds, the Taoiseach (prime minister) of Ireland, resigned. *The Sunday Times* published an article defamatory of him, and he instituted libel proceedings against the newspaper.

Both of the competing interests were important. On the one hand is freedom of expression, a freedom of high importance, on the other hand is protection of reputation. Reputation is an integral and important part of the dignity of the individual and its protection is conducive to the public good. The crux of the appeal lay in identifying the restrictions fairly and reasonably necessary for the protection of reputation.

The solution preferred by the House was for the court to have regard to all the circumstances when deciding whether the publication of particular material was privileged because of its value to the public. This solution had the merit of elasticity. Its disadvantage was an element of unpredictability and uncertainty. This was not to be exaggerated. The common law, I said, does not seek to set a higher standard than that of responsible journalism, a standard the media themselves espouse. An incursion into press freedom which goes no further than this would not seem to be excessive or disproportionate. The elasticity of the common law principle would enable the court to give appropriate weight, in today's conditions, to the importance of freedom of expression by the media on all matters of public concern.

I then set out a non-exhaustive list of ten matters to be taken into account by a court, depending on the circumstances: matters such as the seriousness of the allegation, the steps taken to verify the information, whether comment was sought from the plaintiff, whether the article contained the gist of his side of the story. I concluded:

> 'Above all, the court should have particular regard to the importance of freedom of expression. The press discharges vital functions as a bloodhound as well as a watchdog. The court should be slow to conclude that a publication was not in the public interest and, therefore, the public had no right to know, especially when the information is in the field of political discussion. Any lingering doubts should be resolved in favour of publication.'

The House dismissed the newspaper's appeal, on the ground that, shorn of Mr Reynolds' explanation, the newspaper's serious allegations were not information the public had a right to know.

Having lost its case the defendant newspaper, and the press generally, could not be expected to laud the decision of the House. Nor did they. 'Tiptoeing towards free speech', 'Libel remains a lottery' and 'Our limited freedoms' were typical headlines. The leading article in the *Sunday Times* accused me of continuing to favour 'the muzzle of common law restrictions on free speech'. *The Guardian* was more positive: 'Editors win "right to know" defence in libel.'

Two years later the leading article in the *Times* adopted a more balanced approach, describing my Reynolds judgment as a 'careful but important step towards liberating British libel law from the deadweight of narrow precedent'. The leader writer regrouped my ten tests as, first, whether publication of the article is in the public interest and, secondly, whether the newspaper had acted responsibly and in good faith.

This was encouraging. The Defamation Act 2013 has now enacted, to much the same effect, a statutory defence of 'publication on a matter of public interest' in place of 'the common law defence known as the Reynolds defence'.

My example of a case where change was needed but the cure was beyond the reach of the judges was one of only two occasions I can recall where as many as nine judges sat together on the judicial committee. The appeal was brought to resolve a conflict between two recent decisions, one of the House of Lords and the other of the judicial committee, on the ingredients of the defence of provocation to a charge of murder.

The appeal was from a decision of the Court of Appeal of Jersey where, on the subject under review, the law of Jersey was the same as English law. Decisions on appeals to the judicial committee are binding on the courts of the countries from which the appeals emanated but not elsewhere. So the decision by the judicial committee on this appeal would be binding on the courts of Jersey but, ironically, not on English courts even though the decision would be based on the judicial committee's view of English law on the disputed question. The enlarged board was convened to achieve the result that its decision would be followed by English courts without the need for a separate and later appeal to the House of Lords on the same point of law. This, indeed, is what happened.

For many years the defence, or more accurately, the partial defence of provocation was available to a charge of murder when that offence attracted a mandatory sentence of death. The common law recognised that sometimes the extenuating circumstances in which a person commits murder should reduce his conviction to the lesser, but still very serious, offence of manslaughter.

In 1957 Parliament enacted the Homicide Act, Jersey following suit in 1986 with the Homicide (Jersey) Law. These statutory provisions envisaged that, like the common law, the defence of provocation had two ingredients: first, the factual ingredient of whether the defendant was provoked into losing self-control and, secondly, the objective or evaluative ingredient of whether 'the provocation was enough to make a reasonable man do as he did … [taking] into account everything both done and said according to the effect it would have on a reasonable man.'

The two different judicial views turned on whether, in considering the second ingredient, the jury should take into account any mental or other abnormalities suffered by the defendant. One view was that they could. The jury should apply the standard of self-control to be expected of the particular individual. The other view was that, having assessed the gravity of the provocation to the defendant, the standard of self-control by which his conduct was to be evaluated was the external standard of a person having and exercising ordinary powers of self-control.

In the judicial committee the majority, six law lords, took the view that the former view was a model which could be adopted in framing a law relating to provocation but there was one compelling and overriding reason why this could not be regarded as an accurate statement of English law. I said:

'The law of homicide is a highly sensitive and highly controversial area of the criminal law. In 1957 Parliament altered the common law relating to provocation and declared what the law on this subject thenceforth should be. In these circumstances it is not open to judges now to change ('develop') the common law and thereby depart from the law as declared by Parliament. … The [minority view] involves a significant relaxation of the uniform, objective standard adopted by Parliament. Under the statute the sufficiency of the provocation … is to be judged by one standard, not a standard which varies from defendant to defendant. …The statute does not leave each jury free to set whatever standard they consider appropriate in the circumstances by which to judge whether the defendant's conduct is 'excusable'.'

I added that the majority shared the view of the law commission that the law relating to provocation was flawed to an extent beyond reform by the courts and could not be reformulated in isolation from a review of the law of homicide as a whole.

CHAPTER 25

Not Always Right
Dissenting Judgments

SOMETIMES I WAS unable to persuade my colleagues of the error of their ways. Then I had recourse to a dissenting judgment.

This did not occur often. The records show that in 164 appeals in the House of Lords and the privy council I gave a fully reasoned judgment of my own. Of these only twenty were dissenting judgments. Even this does not give the complete picture because these figures do not include the many appeals in which I simply agreed with my colleagues. Be that as it may, after I had retired, two academic legal scholars, Neal Geach and Christopher Monaghan, invited me to write a foreword to their book *Dissenting Judgments in the Law*. They must have regarded me as something of an expert in this field.

Dissenting judgments are not just an opportunity to let off steam. They can serve as a useful pointer to a different and better outcome and, at best, be taken up by judges in later cases or by Parliament. Some of Lord Denning's famous dissenting judgments led the way forward. So far as I know the only dissenting judgment of mine canonised in this way was a judgment in a privy council appeal from Hong Kong. After the judgments had been given, the procedural rules of courts in England, and possibly also those in Hong Kong, were promptly changed to accord with my interpretation, an interpretation which had been rejected by the majority.

I have selected three of my dissenting judgments as illustrations of this aspect of my work. Inevitably they are a little complicated. If the factual and legal position had been plain and straightforward there would have been no occasion for the judges to reach different conclusions.

The first example concerns the important, if legally complex, case of Mr Gregg who had the misfortune to suffer from cancer. His prospects were uncertain but he had a 45% chance of recovery. Unhappily his doctor negligently misdiagnosed his condition as benign, and the necessary treatment was delayed for months. As a result Mr Gregg lost his chance of recovery. His prospects of recovery became nil or almost nil. The question before the House of Lords was whether Mr Gregg was entitled to an award of damages in respect of his doctor's negligence.

In order to explain the two different views of the judges on this appeal I must start with a brief explanation of the proof of facts in civil cases. If the question before a court is whether a disputed event happened the court proceeds on the basis of the balance of probability. If it is more likely than not, then the event is treated as having happened, if less likely it is treated as not having happened. This is the 'all-or-nothing' balance of probability approach.

The present case is more complicated than that. In the present case the question is what would have happened if a past event (here, the doctor's negligence) had not occurred. In general the same all-or-nothing balance of probability approach is adopted when answering this question.

If this approach is applied in Mr Gregg's case his claim fails. It fails because probably he would not have recovered from his cancer even if he had been treated promptly. This was probable because his prospects of recovery were less than 50%. That was the approach adopted by three law lords when dismissing Mr Gregg's case.

This all-or-nothing balance of probability approach is not always appropriate. Typically this is where the claimant was deprived of an opportunity or chance. Then the law abandons the all-or-nothing approach in favour of valuing, as best it can, the chance or opportunity the claimant lost. For instance, in a case where a solicitor's negligence deprived the claimant of an opportunity to negotiate a better bargain, damages were assessed on the basis of 'loss of a chance'.

This was the approach adopted by Lord Hope of Craighead and me in our dissenting judgments in the present case. Mr Gregg lost his chance of recovery, and damages should be assessed on that basis.

The judgments of the five judges covered seventy-eight close-typed pages of A4 paper. I cannot do more than quote some brief extracts from my own dissenting judgment. Having referred to the approach adopted by the majority I said this:

> 'This surely cannot be the state of the law today. It would be irrational and indefensible. The loss of a 45% prospect of recovery is just as much a real loss for a patient as the loss of a 55% prospect of recovery. In both cases the patient was worse off. He lost something of importance and value. But, it is said, in one case the patient has a claim, in the other he does not.
>
> That would make no sort of sense. It would mean that in the 45% case the doctor's duty would be hollow. The duty would be empty of content … The common law does not compel courts to proceed in such an unreal fashion. I would hold that a patient has a right to a remedy as much where his prospects of recovery were less than 50-50 as where they exceeded 50-50.'

I added:

> 'In these cases a doctor's duty to act in the best interests of his patient involves maximising the patient's recovery prospects, and doing so whether the patient's prospects are good or not so good. In the event of a breach of this duty the law must fashion a matching and meaningful remedy. A patient should have an appropriate remedy when he loses the very thing it was the doctor's duty to protect. To this end the law should recognise the existence and loss of poor and indifferent prospects as well as those more favourable.'

Lord Hope agreed. He said that what had to be valued was what Mr Gregg had lost, and the principle on which that loss should be calculated was the same irrespective of whether the prospects of recovery were better or less than 50%.

My second example concerns liability of a local authority for a share of responsibility for a serious accident between Mr Stovin on his motorcycle and a car driven by Mrs Wise at a dangerously blind corner. The trial judge held Mrs Wise was 70% to blame and the Norfolk County Council 30%. The Court of Appeal dismissed an appeal by the local authority. In the House of Lords, by a majority of three to two, the House upheld a further appeal by the local authority and absolved it from all liability.

The reason the council was involved was this. The council knew this was an exceedingly dangerous junction and that there had been two accidents at this corner. The remedial work could be done quickly, cheaply and effectively. The work would cost less than £1,000 and money was available. The council decided to act and in January 1988 contacted British Rail, the owner of the land, suggesting that part of a bank should be removed to improve visibility. In February 1988 a site meeting took place and the British Rail representatives agreed to seek the necessary internal approval. Then the council let the matter go to sleep, even though a third accident occurred on 6th March 1988. Mr Stovin's accident took place in December 1988, nine months after this third accident and eleven months after the council had decided to act.

In the House of Lords the only question was whether, as a matter of law, the council owed any common law duty of care to Mr Stovin in respect of its admitted negligence.

Liability for omissions (failure to act), as distinct from liability for acts, is a controversial area of the law. Here the local authority did not create the danger. But, as the highway authority, it had responsibility for maintaining and improving this highway including power to remove potential sources of danger. Admittedly, it had failed to discharge its statutory responsibilities with reasonable care.

I said, and this was the crucial step in the elaborate arguments:

> …'.had the authority complied with its public law obligations the danger would have been removed and the accident would never have happened. In such a case the authority can properly be regarded as responsible for the accident just as much as if its employees had carried out roadworks carelessly and thereby created a danger. There is no sensible distinction between an authority's liability for its workmen in the former instance and its liability if, in breach of its public law obligations, office staff fail to do their jobs properly and an avoidable road accident takes place in consequence.'

Lord Slynn of Hadley agreed.

My third example concerns sale of goods and a typical case of fraud. A hire purchase company, in all innocence, hires a car to a crook who claims to be someone else known to be creditworthy. The crook then sells the car to an innocent buyer. When the hire company discovers it has been defrauded, can it reclaim the car from the innocent buyer? The answer is that the company can if, but only if, it had not entered into a contract with the crook.

What happened in the present case was that a crook visited a car dealer's showroom and, claiming to be a Mr Patel, entered into a hire purchase agreement with Mitsubishi Finance for a Mitsubishi Shogun car. The crook sold the car to Mr Hudson who acted throughout in good faith. The crook then vanished without trace. Mitsubishi claimed return of the vehicle. Mr Hudson claimed the crook had passed him a good title under certain provisions of the Hire Purchase Act 1964. The vital question was whether Shogun had entered into a contract with the crook even though it believed the crook was someone else.

In the Court of Appeal Sedley LJ said the law had tied itself into a Gordian knot and a much earlier decision of the House of Lords (*Cundy v Lindsay*) stood in the way of a coherent development of this branch of the law. Brooke LJ said the law was in a 'sorry condition' only Parliament or the House of Lords could remedy. In his judgment in the House of Lords Lord Millett said:

> 'We have the opportunity to restate the law, and cannot shirk the duty of putting it on a basis which is both just and principled, even if it means deciding that we should no longer follow a previous decision of the House. We cannot leave the law as it is. It is neither fair nor principled, and not all the authorities

from which it is derived can be reconciled; some, at least, must be overruled if it is to be extricated from the present quagmire.'

The majority took the view that when Shogun entered into its written hire contract, expressed to be made with Mr Patel, it intended to contract with him and no one else. It never entered into a contract with the crook. So Shogun was entitled to recover its car.

Lord Millett and I dissented. I said:

'The document submitted to Shogun Finance, and signed by the crook in the name of Mr Patel, does of course refer unequivocally to Mr Patel. The document identifies him with some particularity: his full name and address, his date of birth [etc]. These details were of prime importance to Shogun Finance because they identified the person whose credit rating it had checked and approved. The company intended to contract with this person. But it is clear from the evidence that Shogun Finance, as much as the dealer in the car showroom, thought this was one and the same person as the individual in the showroom. Shogun Finance proceeded in this (fraud-induced) belief. In the belief that the person in the dealer's showroom was Mr Patel, Shogun Finance intended to hire the car *to that person*. That is what the finance company intended to do by the written hire-purchase agreement, and that is what it thought it had done. Had this not been so it would not have released the car to him. Shogun Finance was mistaken in its belief about the identity of the person in the showroom … But that mistaken belief, induced by the crook's fraudulent misrepresentation, did not negative the finance company's intention to let the car on hire to the person in the showroom on the terms set out in the hire-purchase agreement.'

Lord Millett's judgment was to the same effect. Both of us reviewed and analysed the present state of the law with some care, and we both agreed that the decision in *Cundy v Lindsay* should no longer be followed. The majority found it unnecessary to undertake such a review or express any views on the *Cundy v Lindsay* decision. So the appeal did nothing to clear up the mess.

CHAPTER 26

Never Say Never
Decisions for Tomorrow

SOMETIMES AN APPEAL raises, or touches upon, a controversial issue of major importance which, as matters proceed, need not be decided. Then, without deciding the point, the House may wish to keep the issue alive for decision on a future occasion. I give two examples.

The first case concerned a company called Spectrum, a paint manufacturer. In 1997 the company granted a charge over its book debts to a bank as security for an overdraft. Spectrum's business failed and it went into liquidation. The question before the court was whether the bank's charge was 'floating' or 'fixed'. If the former, Spectrum's preferential creditors, including the Inland Revenue, had priority over the bank, if the latter they did not. In 1979, some twenty years earlier, a High Court judge had decided that this form of charge created a fixed charge, and on this appeal the Inland Revenue challenged the correctness of this decision. This charge was in the bank's normal form, and over the years many other banks and commercial lenders had used a similar form.

The law lords decided the earlier decision was wrong. The bank urged the House, having regard to the earlier erroneous court decision, to direct that its decision should apply only to debentures entered into in future. The decision of the House should not apply to existing debentures.

'Prospective overruling', as this is called, has had a mixed reception throughout common law countries. The traditional approach in this country is that when a court ruling changes the law from what it was previously thought to be, the change operates retrospectively as well as prospectively. Lord Reid, an eminent law lord in the 1950s and 1960s, observed, 'we cannot say the law was one thing yesterday but it is to be something different tomorrow.'

In the Spectrum case I said that, constitutionally, in an appropriate case the judges do have power to modify the established practice and direct that the court ruling in that case shall apply only to the future and not be retrospective:

> 'If, altogether exceptionally, the House as the country's supreme court were
> to follow this course I would not regard it as trespassing outside the functions

properly to be discharged by the judiciary under this country's constitution. Rigidity in the operation of a legal system is a sign of weakness, not strength. It deprives a legal system of necessary elasticity. Far from achieving a constitutionally exemplary result, it can produce a legal system unable to function effectively in changing times. 'Never say never' is a wise precept, in the interests of all citizens of the country.'

I added an encouraging note that, since the Strasbourg court interprets and applies the European Convention of Human Rights with prospective effect only, it would be odd if in interpreting and applying Convention rights the House was not able to give rulings having a comparable limited temporal effect.

My conclusion, in agreement with my colleagues, was that the present case was 'miles away' from the exceptional category in which alone prospective overruling would be legitimate.

So the prospective overruling issue has been raised and remains to be decided on another day.

An even more important constitutional issue was raised, but left unresolved, in the 'hunting' case of Jackson in 2005. The question before the House concerned, quite exceptionally, the validity of an Act of Parliament. The Hunting Act 2004 banned hunting foxes with dogs. The legal challenge was not based on the content of the new Act. The challenge was based on the parliamentary procedure by which this Act had reached the statute book. The Hunting Act was not enacted in the usual way with the consent of both Houses of Parliament. The Hunting Act was enacted with the consent of the House of Commons but without the consent of the House of Lords. This was done pursuant to the provisions of the Parliament Act 1911 as amended by the Parliament Act 1949.

In these proceedings the claimants asserted that this procedure was flawed. In order to explain the flaw I must first say something about the Parliament Acts of 1911 and 1949.

The background to the 1911 Act is well known. Early in the 20th century the political imbalance of the two Houses of Parliament gave rise to a prolonged constitutional crisis. The legislative programme of successive Liberal governments was thwarted time and again by sustained opposition from the Conservative and Unionist dominated House of Lords. Matters came to a head with the rejection of Lloyd George's Finance Bill ('the people's budget') of 1909. A government cannot govern without the supply of money.

The crisis was eventually resolved by the Parliament Act 1911, passed by the House of Lords under overt threat from the government to create sufficient Liberal peers to achieve the Bill's passage through the Lords if opposition in that House continued. In short the effect of this Act was that a Bill rejected by the House of Lords in three consecutive sessions could receive the Royal Assent without further ado, provided two years had elapsed between its second reading in the first of those sessions in the House of Commons and the date when it passed the House of Commons in the third of those sessions.

The new procedure was then used to enact two important constitutional measures: the Government of Ireland Act 1914 and the Welsh Church Act 1914.

In 1949 the Parliament Act of that year amended the 1911 Act by further limiting the powers of the House of Lords. The 1949 Act reduced from three to two the number of sessions in which a Bill had to pass the House of Commons and from three to two the number of years which had to elapse. This Act, and this step is of critical importance, was not enacted with the consent of both Houses of Parliament. It was enacted with the consent only of the House of Commons, in accordance with the abbreviated procedure set up by the 1911 Act. This meant that this abbreviated procedure, effectually increasing the powers of the House of Commons in 1911, was being used as a means to increase further the powers of that House.

This was the crux of the claimants' submissions. Their case was that the enlarged power given to the House of Commons by the 1911 Act did not enable the Commons to enlarge its own powers still further. Otherwise the limitations set in place by the 1911 statute would be meaningless. A power given in limited terms cannot be used to enlarge itself. Further restriction on the power of the House of Lords required its consent.

I pause to note that, if this submission were well founded, the consequence would be that the Hunting Act was invalid because the procedure by which it was enacted was flawed.

All the law lords rejected this argument. My view was that, as a matter of interpretation of the 1911 Act, no restriction on the scope of the new procedure was implicit. Ministerial statements made in Parliament during the parliamentary passage of the Bill for the 1911 Act made this plain, and the 1949 Act procedure has subsequently been used to enact several statutes, each of which has itself been recognised and treated as valid in later statutes enacted with the consent of both Houses.

The matters raised but left open for another occasion were these. In the course of his submissions the Attorney General said the government might wish to use the 1949 Act to bring about constitutional changes such as altering the composition of the House of Lords. Logically the Act could be used to abolish the House of Lords altogether. This submission prompted some cautionary words from Lord Steyn on the limits of parliamentary sovereignty today:

> 'In exceptional circumstances involving judicial review or the ordinary role of the courts, the … new Supreme Court may have to consider whether this is a constitutional fundamental which even a sovereign Parliament acting at the behest of a complaisant House of Commons cannot abolish.'

Lord Hope of Craighead added a forceful observation:

> 'Parliamentary sovereignty is no longer, if it ever was, absolute. … Step by step, gradually but surely, the English principle of the absolute legislative sovereignty of Parliament which Dicey derived from Coke and Blackstone is being qualified … The rule of law enforced by the courts is the ultimate controlling factor on which our constitution is based.'

Baroness Hale of Richmond observed that the courts 'will treat with particular suspicion (and might even reject) any attempt to subvert the rule of law by removing governmental action affecting the rights of the individual from all judicial scrutiny.'

It is devoutly to be hoped that these observations will never need to be tested.

CHAPTER 27

Travelling Again
More Law Abroad

JENNY AND I made several interesting overseas visits. In 1994 I was invited by the Law Council of Australia to deliver a lecture at its 1995 superannuation conference. The chosen subject was the extent to which trustees can have regard to ethical considerations when exercising their investment powers. This invitation, no doubt, arose from the fact that in 1992 as vice-chancellor I had decided a case brought by the bishop of Oxford who, unsuccessfully, challenged the investment policy of the Church Commissioners.

We visited Australia in February 1995. We spent one week in Sydney, staying in comfort in Double Bay. We travelled to the city centre by a delightful twenty minutes' sail to and from Circular Quay. In the course of the conference, as I was resuming my seat after an interval, the chairman said to me and others, 'hurry along please, take your seats now.' The chairman, who was a High Court judge, then added for the benefit of the whole conference: 'I never thought I would have the opportunity to tell a law lord to sit down.'

We spent our second week in Melbourne where I addressed a different group of lawyers at a seminar on 'Current Developments in Equity'. My contribution was titled 'Inequity in Equity'. We were delighted to be able to visit Anthony and Gina Bailey at their home.

In both cities we received generous hospitality. We had an opportunity to see some of the sights, to sail around the marvellous harbour in Sydney, and enjoy the Australian sunshine in the middle of the English winter. On one occasion in Sydney we were relaxing alone on the beach at Manly when, suddenly and silently, at our feet a large party of Japanese divers arose en masse out of the sea carrying what looked like spears. For a moment we thought an invasion was taking place, but they proved to be harmless.

The next stop was the Cayman Islands. Before his retirement in 1994 Lord Templeman was patron of the Cayman Islands law school, and I succeeded him in this office. This was particularly apt, as this law school was affiliated to Liverpool University and its degrees were the law degrees of that university.

On The Bench

We made two trips to Cayman, in August 1995 and in August 1998. The purpose of these visits was to present degree certificates and prizes to the graduates, coupled with appropriate congratulatory sentiments and good wishes.

Jenny and I were thoroughly spoiled on both visits. Our first visit was for a brief three days, so we were kept quite busy. Our initial commitment on the first day was to collect a hire car kindly arranged for us. I was surprised to find that the car, like all the cars on the island, had an automatic engine. Until then the only cars I had driven had manual gear change. However we survived, helped by the fact that on Grand Cayman there is a low speed limit.

Then the social round took over. In the evening we were guests at a reception given by chief justice Harre with his fellow Grand Court judges and their itinerant Court of Appeal judges who chanced to be in Cayman that weekend. On the second day we attended a celebratory graduation dinner given by the students' society. On the next day we lunched with the governor and his wife at Government House.

In the course of the lunch I contrived to commit a faux pas. I understood from other sources that the governor was very keen on birds. 'Oh,' I said to him, thinking to air my (non-existent) expertise, 'are you a twitcher or a birdee?' His Excellency looked pained. 'Neither,' he said, 'I am an ornithologist.' It was only later I learned that he was a world renowned leader in this field.

The graduation ceremony took place in the evening. Like all prizegivings, it was a relaxed and agreeable occasion, with smiles all round. We were made welcome by Mitchell Davies, the director of studies at the law school, and everyone else.

During our short stay we stayed at a splendid hotel across the road from the glorious Seven Mile Beach. So we found time in the mornings to cross the road and have a quick dip in the wonderfully blue-green sea with the sun blazing down. Out at sea, on our last morning, were several impressive waterspouts.

On our second visit we stayed for longer, this time for a full week. Early in 1998 I had been careless enough to succumb to a severe attack of bronchial hyperactivity. The chance of relaxing for a few days in the clean air and warm sunshine of the Caribbean was an opportunity not to be lost.

The programme was much the same as on our previous visit, only this time there was a new governor. I was invited to appear on the Islands' radio, but when I found I would need to be in the studio by 6am I had no difficulty in declining.

The only novel activity was that, after I had completed my commitments, one morning we went down in a submarine to gaze at the colourful fish and coral. I was keen to do this, Jenny was not. But she insisted on accompanying me to whatever fate was in store. She is now, according to the 'certificate' we were given after we surfaced again, an 'Atlantis Submariner'.

That was in 1998. It was our last visit although I continued as patron until 2006.

In September 1999 I was fortunate indeed to be co-opted as a member of a remarkable visit to Paris by a delegation of senior English judges. The driving force behind the visit was Professor Basil Markesinis, now Sir Basil. He was the director of the Institute of European and Comparative Law of Oxford University. The underlying aim of the trip was to further the affairs of this institute. I was fortunate, not least because I have no connection with that university.

Basil Markesinis assembled an impressive array of judges. The other six were Lord Goff of Chieveley (senior lord of appeal), Lord Bingham (lord chief justice), Lord Woolf (master of the rolls), Sir Robert Carswell (lord chief justice of Northern Ireland), Lord Clyde (law lord) and Sir Peter Gibson (lord justice of appeal). In addition were Ross Cranston (solicitor general), Martin Matthews (chairman of the Oxford faculty board of law), Keith Clark (senior partner of Clifford Chance) and John Brown (managing partner of Clifford Chance Paris). Together with our wives we were a large party.

The programme was hectic. We got off to a jolly start. We boarded our Eurostar train at Waterloo station to the accompaniment of the strains of 'Yellow Submarine' played by a brass band on the platform. It was the first time we had used this train and been through the Channel tunnel. In Paris we stayed at the Hotel Raphael, near the Champs Élysées. We reached there about 5pm, and were quickly on duty. At 6pm we attended a conference in the Grands Salons at the Sorbonne, where the proceedings were largely conducted in French. This was followed by a reception. That was our first day.

On the following day we started early, with a working breakfast at 8.30am with the president of the National Assembly, M Laurent Fabius. 'Working' it may have been but there was very little breakfast. We were then whisked to the Élysée Palace to be received at noon by the president of France, M Chirac, and photographed with him. The reception lasted about one hour. It was fascinating, but nothing of substance was discussed. This was, I think, a diplomatic formality.

By now we were feeling the heat. So it was good to relax over an excellent lunch. We were on duty again later in the afternoon. We met the foreign minister at 4.30pm, and from that we were driven straight to a reception – standing again – given by the minister of justice Mme Guigou. That kept us occupied until 7pm.

We returned to our hotel for a quick change for a dinner party at the British Embassy, starting at 8pm. For this function the men were joined by their wives.

Meeting President Chirac.

They had spent the day visiting Monet's garden at Giverny. That, too, had been a tiring day.

The embassy was intriguing. It could not fail to be so for anybody who has read Nancy Mitford's novel *Don't Tell Alfred*. As would be expected, the meal itself was excellent, although the French guests seemed to make a point of speaking French even though their English was much better than my French.

On the next day the wives had a 'free day'. The men had a session from 10am to 11.30am with judges at the Conseil d'État. We then moved on to lunch with the president of the Conseil Constitutionel, followed in the afternoon by a meeting with the full council.

Our time was then our own until we returned to England at noon next day. Jenny and I made a brief shopping expedition to the Champs Élysées.

Overall, for the men in particular, it was a unique experience, meeting people we would not otherwise have met and seeing inside buildings otherwise closed to us.

On 31st December 2000 Jenny and I flew to India. Our destination was Calcutta but by the time we arrived, shortly after midnight, its name had changed to Kolkata. It was an unusual flight. Being New Year's Eve the plane was virtually empty. I have never travelled on an aeroplane with so few passengers. As we drove to our accommodation in Kolkata the streets were alive with fires and celebrations. We stayed at the Bengal club, a social club founded in 1827. The clubhouse was built in the colonial style.

The purpose of the visit was for me to give a lecture, the second Sarkar lecture, at the British council. Gordon Slynn had delivered the first lecture. Our host was Mr Sudipto Sarkar. He was the fourth successive generation in a family renowned for its legal scholarship.

The lecture was planned for 3rd January, so we had two days in hand. We had arranged this interval to give ourselves time to recover from the lengthy flight. In fact, unexpectedly, the gap gave us time to go to the Calcutta races. These races were firmly established as a feature of New Year's Day. They were great fun. Our hostess Malabika took much care to see we did not eat anything likely to upset us.

On the following day we explored something of Kolkata. Until 1912 Calcutta, as it was then known, was the administrative capital of India. It was also the commercial and industrial capital. Much of the city, especially on the banks of the river Hooghly, was a densely populated slum area. We drove across the famous Hooghly bridge and beside some of the narrow lanes and crowded bazaars.

Some handsome buildings, Victorian and earlier, still survived. The cathedral and the marble Queen Victoria memorial are situated on the Maidan, a fine grass-covered park. We strolled across the park and into these buildings. It was all quite nostalgic, not least when in the cathedral we saw a statue erected in memory of Bishop Heber, the second bishop of Calcutta.

This fine statue reminded us of John Waterson in St Mary's church in Stoke D'Abernon. When in the course of a service he announced the next hymn his practice was to say a few words about the author and the music. John was fond of nature hymns. One of these was an evocative hymn sung to an attractive lively traditional English melody: '*When spring unlocks the flowers to paint the laughing soil…*' The author was Bishop Heber. In a few words John conjured up a picture of the bishop sitting in the heat of Calcutta and remembering the English spring. The bishop died there at the young age of 42 years. And here we were, standing in the same place and the self-same heat, pondering how he must have felt when writing this hymn.

I interpose a reflection on how times have changed. Bishop Heber was a gifted man. He wrote over fifty hymns, many of which are still sung. My generation will be familiar with the missionary hymn with the opening lines: '*From Greenland's icy mountains, from India's coral strands*'. This hymn, and the accompanying music bearing the name 'Calcutta', were composed by Bishop Heber. This hymn could not be sung in any church today, containing as it does lines such as '*the heathen in his blindness bows down to wood and stone!*' (sic). This is no criticism of an enlightened and progressive priest, who was highly regarded and possessed of much good sense and humanity. Rather it is a reminder that, to greater or lesser extent, we are all products of our time and environment.

Next day we assembled at the offices of the British Council. Jenny was intrigued to meet a couple of elderly Indian ladies who were old Girtonians. My lecture was titled 'Political Reputations and Free Speech', in which I attempted a brief survey of the laws of the principal Commonwealth countries. Afterwards we were entertained at a party given by our hosts.

Our original plan had been to make a quick visit to Darjeeling. Unfortunately visits there were temporarily 'out of bounds'. So we turned our attention to the other end of India: Shimla. We had no difficulty in reaching Delhi, nor in catching an onward plane to Chandigarh. Then the troubles started. Due to thick fog we were unable to land. The plane circled around for a couple of hours and then gave up and returned to Delhi.

The weather forecast was not encouraging. Malabika Sarkar came to our rescue. She arranged for a car to drive us to Shimla next day. Which is the way, frayed around the edges, we eventually reached Shimla, having survived the traffic in Delhi and the winding roads, lined with curious monkeys, up and up to Shimla at an altitude of about 8,000ft. We were worn out.

Shimla lies in the south-western ranges of the Himalayas. Despite being difficult to reach, over 1,000 miles away from Calcutta, this was the summer capital of the British Raj from the 1860s.

British Shimla extended about a mile and a half along a ridge between two hills. On our trip pre-independence structures still abounded. We visited, but were unable to enter, the former Viceregal Lodge. Most of the buildings along the Mall, the main street, were shabby, save for the army barracks. Adjoining the parade ground at one end of the Mall was an Anglican church with Victorian stained glass windows. A service was in progress and we looked inside. The congregation was singing a hymn to a familiar tune, but we soon slipped away. The service was being conducted in a language, presumably Hindi, we could not follow. As we looked around us we were surprised how slowly we were walking. We attributed this to the high altitude.

A notable feature of Shimla was the abundance of monkeys. In our hotel we were advised to keep our room windows firmly shut, otherwise the monkeys would sneak in and steal. They certainly were bold. As it was, they habitually sat on the outside windowsills and peered in through the glass. On one occasion as we were walking along a roadway lined with trees the man in front of us had some candy in his hand behind his back. In a flash a monkey came down a tree and crept behind him and whisked the candy out of his hand and was gone.

We returned to Delhi by car. We were not altogether surprised to find that Delhi was still embraced in thick fog. Next morning I was agreeably surprised, and much relieved, that the fog had lifted and our return flight was able to take off without delay. A happy end to a memorable visit.

CHAPTER 28

Middle Temple Treasurer: 1997

I HAVE BEEN a student or member or bencher of the Middle Temple for sixty years. For thirty-five years I worked, as a barrister or judge, within a stone's throw of the Inn. For twenty-five years Jenny and I had a flat within the environs of the Inn.

With this long and close connection it is not surprising I was delighted and honoured when my fellow benchers elected me treasurer for the year 1997.

This nomenclature is misleading. It stems from the original function of the office. In the 16th century the treasurer was responsible for financial matters, collecting dues and so on. Gradually, while retaining the same title, his responsibilities widened and he assumed a degree of pre-eminence over his fellow benchers during his year of office. In modern terminology he is the president of the Inn. A similar transition took place in each of the other Inns of Court.

Before proceeding further into this legal world I should explain that the 'benchers', called masters of the bench irrespective of their sex, resemble fellows of an Oxbridge college. They are the governing body of the Inn and are self-perpetuating. The treasurer presides at formal meetings of benchers. To this day these meetings are known as 'parliaments', another anachronism.

I should also clarify one of the functions of the treasurer: calling to the Bar student members who have passed the necessary examinations and kept the prescribed number of dining terms. The treasurer does so by declaiming to each student in turn 'in the name of the Bench I call you to the degree of the Utter Bar'. When I was called to the Bar I thought that, since 'utter' means 'outer', this was drawing a distinction between junior barristers and QCs who are called to take their seats 'within the Bar'. Apparently this is not so. The expression reflects a practice, long since gone, when law student education took the form of practical exercises, even then known as mooting. The most junior students, who sat on the middle tiers of benches, were known as 'inner barristers'. This appears to be the origin, in the mid-fifteenth century, of the term 'barrister'. The more learned sat outer or 'utter'-most. Call to the utter Bar was recognition of a degree of learning.

On The Bench

The Middle Temple is one of the four Inns of Court which have the right to call students to the Bar. They were founded in the 14th century. The Middle Temple occupies part of the land in the Temple once occupied by the Knights Templars, one of whose seals, Agnus Dei, became the emblem of the Middle Temple. The circular 'round' in the Temple church stands as a reminder that in its origin this was one of the Templar 'round' churches, all of which were based on the configuration of the church of the Holy Sepulchre in Jerusalem.

To a significant extent the office of treasurer is what the holder chooses to make it. Some treasurers are passive and reactive, others proactive. I embarked on the office conscious of continuing uncertainty about the role of an Inn of Court at the end of the 20th century. I was also aware there was room for improvement in the administration of the Inn. I was anxious to make progress under both these headings, even though I was continuing to work full-time as a lord of appeal. I appreciated that in one year very little could be finalised but I felt we must make a start.

On the first point I initiated a series of discussions under the title 'The Inn in a changing world'. Four highly regarded benchers prepared discussion papers on different aspects of the Inn's activities. These were circulated in advance of four parliaments. Towards the end of the year, in a final discussion paper, I sought to sum up the position overall together with some recommendations. Nearly all these recommendations were accepted by parliament.

Disappointingly, but perhaps not surprisingly, after I had left office very few were implemented. One of the small changes which was implemented, and that was done whilst I was still treasurer, was to permit the general public to have access to the Inn's gardens in the summer. I have sometimes reflected, ruefully, that this was the only mark I left on the Inn.

The Inn's standing orders were revised, and some aspects of the financial administration were put on a better footing, but much remained to be done. The Inn's affairs included managing an income flow of about £8 million and maintaining and updating a substantial number of period buildings, including the Temple Church and the Middle Temple hall. The Inn was coping with a financial deficit and suffered from the handicap that benchers largely comprise practising barristers and judges who, inevitably, lack experience in running a business.

More cheerful was the social side of the Inn's activities. Dining has always been a feature of the life of the Inns of Court. This still continues, if somewhat emasculated. Dining terms are still kept by students, and private guest nights continue. The highlight of the dining programme is the annual Grand Day. The treasurer then invites a number of distinguished guests of his choice to a white tie dinner. The guests always included the treasurer's wife and the treasurers of the other Inns. My Grand Day dinner was a splendid occasion in October 1997. The other Inns reciprocated during the year.

Customarily one of the 'perks' of the treasurer is to nominate two honorary benchers. I selected chief justice Andrew Li, from Hong Kong, and the bishop of London. I duly welcomed them. Also in my year the two Inns in the Temple jointly entertained the lord mayor of London and the aldermen and sheriffs at a dinner in the Middle Temple. That was a colourful evening. Both were delightful occasions, but both called for the preparation of yet more speeches.

Another speech I was only too happy to make was at a dinner marking Lord Wilberforce's ninetieth birthday. I have always had much admiration for him and celebrating his birthday was a great pleasure. He retaliated later in the year.

Traditionally each Inn has a royal bencher. In 1997 the Middle Temple had two, the Queen Mother and Diana, Princess of Wales. For some years, unfailingly, the Queen Mother honoured the Inn by dining with the benchers at a 'Family' dinner. Invariably she was on sparkling form.

In August, tragically, Princess Diana died in a car accident in Paris. Jenny and I were invited to her funeral in Westminster Abbey. That was an extraordinary day. From our flat we walked to the abbey along the embankment. Amazingly there was complete and utter silence. We saw not one single car. Hushed crowds lined Parliament Square, but we had no difficulty in obtaining passage through them. We had plain white tickets for the abbey. We assumed we would be seated in some innocuous corner. Instead we were shown to seats in the chancel, one row above the choir. I sat next to Edward Heath.

The service had many poignant moments. The first was when the young princes came in and took their seats. Others were when the burly guardsmen brought in the coffin and, later, Elton John's rendering of Bernie Taupin's 'Candle in the Wind': '*Goodbye England's rose…*' For me the most traumatic moment was at the end of the service when the soldiers lifted the coffin and carried it out of the abbey to the haunting strains of Sir John Tavener's anthem 'Song for Athene' intoned by the processing choir.

With Jenny's support I represented the Inn at several memorial services, including services for Eustace Roskill (Lord Roskill) in Winchester cathedral and Lord Taylor of Gosforth, formerly lord chief justice, in a packed St Paul's cathedral. Peter Taylor was a keen musician and no mean pianist himself. The music at his service included as an anthem 'In paradisum' from Fauré's requiem mass. This beautiful music is always appropriate on these occasions when, as at St Paul's, there is a suitable choir at hand.

Greeting the Queen Mother.

Jenny greeting the Lord Mayor.

My predecessor as treasurer was Michael Sherrard QC. He was responsible for introducing advocacy training to the Inn. Previously this was thought incapable of being taught by instruction. Each year he took a small party of Inn students plus some benchers to Cumberland Lodge, in Windsor Great Park, for a weekend training session. Jenny and I dutifully presented ourselves at the session held in March 1997.

On Sunday morning most of the party attended a church service at the Royal Chapel in the park. After the service the Queen Mother invited our Middle Temple party to her home in Royal Lodge for a drink. In her home we were joined by the Queen and several other royals. This was an unforgettable occasion. Everybody was relaxed and chatty in this domestic environment with, I remember, masses of flowers on all sides.

At the final parliament in a treasurer's year of office one of the senior benchers thanks the outgoing treasurer for his labours. In my case Richard Wilberforce performed this task. He enjoyed himself by teasing me for having failed in my attempt to abolish the office of Master of the Snuff.

Dining the Lord Mayor in Middle Temple hall.

The fountain in the Middle Temple, by Joseph Nicholls, active 1726–55.

CHAPTER 29

A Coat Of Arms
Let Equity Prevail: 1995

WHEN I SAW 'Garter' concerning my title as a peer he asked if I would be interested in having a coat of arms. As a peer I would be entitled to include two supporters, which always add interest to the overall 'achievement'.

Nowadays personal coats of arms are an absurd anachronism. But they can be fun. Displayed at home as colourful accessories they provide an unusual talking point. They have little place in the wider world. The Inns of Court are among the few exceptions. In the Middle Temple the arms of the treasurers, stretching back to the end of the 16th century, are displayed in the hall or, now there is no space on the walls of the hall, in one of the corridors. Jenny and I decided to go ahead.

Heraldry is a world of its own with its own language and rules. So we had to start from scratch in choosing the elements of my coat of arms. Essentially a personal coat of arms ('an armorial achievement') comprises, starting at the bottom, a shield ('an escutcheon'), a helmet ('helm') and a crest with mantling. The supporters stand on either side of the shield. Below the shield is the bearer's motto. The strict rule about mixing colours ('tincture') was originally aimed at providing contrast and visibility. Today this serves to give a coat of arms a distinct tone. The two metals, gold and silver, generally light in colour, cannot be placed on each other. Nor may any of the other colours be laid on each other. The word 'supporters' suggests people but Garter advised that, artistically, birds or animals make the best supporters. Dragons, apparently, are reserved for royalty.

Armed with this guidance Jenny and I sat down to compile a list of suggestions. The ultimate product, expressed in non-heraldic language, was this. The central item, the shield, is black and gold reflecting the robes of a lord justice, with birch leaves as a reference to Birkenhead. Above the shield and helm is a baron's coronet and, above that, a crest and mantling in black and gold. Then a mole, an allusion to the river Mole near which we have lived for so long. In its paws the mole is holding, ever so gently, a golden daffodil, a reference to Jenny's Welsh ancestry. The supporters are two black cormorants, reminders of the well-known liver birds on the clock towers at Liverpool's pier head. The badge, which can be worn by any

Coat of Arms.

member of the family, is a mole grasping a daffodil between its forepaws within a garland of birch leaves.

We had more difficulty in selecting a motto. Mottos vary widely. Some are buried in history, others are a play on a name. Lawyers often choose a motto having a reference to justice, such as Lord Denning's '*Fiat justitia*'. I settled on 'Let Equity Prevail', an imperative phrase with a double meaning. Most mottos are written in Latin, but the combined linguistic skills of the family were unable to produce a suitable translation.

In this motto the word equity is a synonym for fairness. This epitomises my legal philosophy. Behind this primary and obvious meaning is a secondary meaning, apparent only to lawyers. As mentioned earlier, judge-made law has two separate strands: common law and equity. Until 1875 these laws were administered in separate courts: the common law courts and the Court of Chancery. When the administration of the two sets of law was fused in 1875 the statute provided that where there was any conflict or variance between the rules of equity and those of the common law 'the rules of equity shall prevail'. As a barrister and a High Court judge I had worked in the Chancery Division. This motto was a light-hearted reminder to common lawyers to keep them in their place.

The actual grant of the arms, signed by garter principal king of arms on behalf of the earl marshal, is an elaborate document. In my grant the attractive border was based on a wrought iron type of design with birch leaves, a suggestion made by Jenny. Within six little windows are symbolic references to features in my life: the crescent of Trinity Hall, the Paschal Lamb of the Middle Temple, the scales of justice, the rose from a ceiling boss in St Mary's church, the portcullis emblem of the House of Lords, the escallop-shell of St James.

In 1998 Peter Gwynn-Jones published a book, *The Art of Heraldry*. I was delighted to find, prominent among the illustrations, a whole page extract from my grant showing both the coat of arms and 'Jenny's' border.

CHAPTER 30

The End Of The Law Lords
The New Supreme Court

THE ABOLITION OF the lords of appeal is a sorry, unedifying story. The new Supreme Court was conceived in haste and had a difficult period of gestation. But ultimately a healthy baby was born in October 2009 and since then it has thrived.

The background was that in 1999 a royal commission was set up to consider reform of the House of Lords ('A House for the Future'). The commission reported in January 2000 and concluded there was insufficient reason to change the present arrangements regarding the law lords. 'Indeed', the commission said, 'we see some advantage in having senior judges in the legislature where they can be made aware of the social developments and political balances which underlie most legislation.' The commission recommended that the 'lords of appeal in ordinary should continue to be ex officio members of the reformed second chamber and carry out its judicial functions.'

In June 2000, in accordance with a recommendation of the royal commission, Lord Bingham announced in the chamber of the House of Lords the principles the lords of appeal intended to observe when participating in debates and votes in the chamber and when considering their eligibility to sit on related cases.

Following this, in November 2001 the government's white paper on House of Lords reform was 'committed to maintaining judicial membership of the House of Lords' and that law lords 'should continue to be members of the Lords until aged seventy-five whether or not they sit judicially.'

It was in this setting that on 12th June 2003, out of the blue, the government announced it was introducing legislation to set up a new supreme court and, as part of a cabinet reshuffle, had abolished the office of lord chancellor. This announcement was made without any prior consultation and without even the courtesy of notifying in advance those most concerned. In this brutal fashion the government sacked the existing lord chancellor, Lord Irvine of Lairg. He learned of his dismissal through the media.

This was a singularly unfortunate start. *The Guardian* newspaper, in a leading article, described these 'important changes' as having been launched 'with staggering ineptitude'. In an article in the *Times* William Rees-Mogg castigated the prime minister:

'Nothing has been worse handled by the prime minister than his judicial reforms. He did not consult the law lords; he did not consult the lord chief justice; he could not get the past lord chancellor's agreement; he did not perform his constitutional duty to tell the Queen. He mixed up the most important judicial reform in a century with a panic reshuffle of his cabinet. He thought he had abolished the office of lord chancellor, which he did not have the power to do.

The new lord chancellor, Lord Falconer of Thoroton, who had thought he would never have to act as lord chancellor, had to borrow an ill-fitting wig and will have to buy black tights. This was the way in which Tony Blair tried to abolish the ancient office of lord chancellor, to create a supreme court of the United Kingdom and to change the method of appointing judges. No deliberation, no forethought, no debate, no consultation.'

This unhappy start had an unsatisfactory consequence. In the normal course a government would be expected to make a decision on a constitutional change of this character only after it had first sought and weighed contrary views. The course followed by this government precluded any such objective exercise. Having announced its intention to create a new supreme court the government could not be expected thereafter to have an open mind on the issue. There were some voices calling for change but no one suggested the existing system did not work. Indeed the royal commission had suggested otherwise.

The government's proposals attracted much criticism, not only from lawyers. The lords of appeal as a whole were divided. Tom Bingham was firmly in favour of the new court and had made his view known. I was unhappy with the proposed change. In December 2003 I wrote an article in the barristers' magazine *Counsel*, described by the *Times* as 'a damning critique'. In a speech in the House of Lords, at an early stage in a six-hour debate, I gave my reasons for preferring the status quo:

'The proposal [to abolish the office of lord of appeal in ordinary] is that, lest our continuing membership of your Lordships' House be misunderstood by anyone, we shall all be taken away to a place of safety in our very own judicial ivory tower that will be purpose built or, at least, specially selected.

I regret that this proposal, put forward with the best of intentions, is misguided because it is unnecessary and would do more harm than good. It is unnecessary because it would achieve nothing of real value. Under the present arrangements the law lords do not lack independence from government. No one suggests that they do. They also do not lack independence from the legislature. Only law lords participate in the judicial business of the House, as all your Lordships know. No one could suggest that in itself the law lords' membership of your Lordships' House compromises our judicial independence in some way.

The proposed change would be harmful because, first, a new supreme court would be deprived of some of the advantages of the present arrangements. At present, the court of final appeal in this country is known throughout the common law world as, simply, the 'House of Lords'. By reason of its long and distinguished history that is still a name to be conjured with. That would be lost. A new court would be just that: a new court. It would be distinct and different from its predecessors. It would have to start from scratch and build up its own reputation under a new name in a new place which inevitably would lack the instant recognition of the Palace of Westminster and the impact this always has on those who come here on judicial business.

There would be another loss, not so immediately obvious but none the less real. When I was summoned to your Lordships' House ten years ago I had been sitting for some years as a judge in the Royal Courts of Justice in the Strand. Like all law courts they are judge-centred. When I came here I immediately became aware of the wider perspective afforded by working daily in an environment which is not judge-centred. Involvement, formal and informal, in the non-judicial business of the House – serving on committees, attending debates when possible and so on – raises the law lords' awareness of the broader context in which legislation and policies are formulated. The law lords benefit from that. It extends their horizons.

Of course that is not essential or indispensable. The judges of a new supreme court would manage without it, as do judges in supreme courts in other countries. But that is not a good reason for us deliberately to choose to abandon something of value which, unlike those other countries, we have.

Another practical drawback with the proposed exile of the law lords is that suitable ivory towers do not come cheaply…

So it will be asked why the law lords are divided on the issue if the arguments are as one-sided and compelling as I suggest. The stumbling block for some is that judges whose responsibility it is to interpret and administer the law should not be able also to participate in making the law. They are two separate functions that should be kept apart. What was acceptable in the past will not pass muster today. Standards have changed.

That argument, expressed as a general principle, is not without attraction. But I part company from those who seek to apply that principle to the position of the law lords in that I am an unrepentant pragmatist on this matter. The present system works. Everyone accepts that. Of course the law lords must be careful not to prejudice their ability to discharge their judicial functions effectively and properly. But the position of the law lords is not unique in this respect. All judges have to be watchful over their extra-judicial activities. That is where we draw the line in this country and it works.

Moreover there is no lack of transparency. The general principles applied by the law lords in deciding whether to participate in the legislative business of the House were reported to the House by the senior law lord in June 2000.

Other countries order their affairs differently. We should not fear to be different. What we should fear is sacrificing on the altar of conformity a valuable feature of our constitutional heritage which has worked so well and still does. I believe the law lords will be better placed to serve this country if they continue as they are.'

At a later stage of the debate Lord Donaldson of Lymington, a former master of the rolls, described my speech as 'devastating'.

Feelings ran high. There was a real possibility that in the House of Lords combined opposition from the Conservatives and cross-benchers would defeat the proposals. In March 2004 the leader of the House of Commons, Peter Hain, threatened to withdraw the Constitutional Reform Bill from the Lords and reintroduce it in the House of Commons and invoke the Parliament Act if the Bill was not passed before the next election.

Lord Lloyd of Berwick, formerly a lord of appeal, masterminded an opposition campaign with consummate skill but ultimately without success. Two features of the third reading of the Bill, in which I spoke again, were critical. First, the debate took place immediately before Christmas: on Monday 20th December 2004. The government's supporters were better self-disciplined in their attendance at a heavy debate in such an unpopular week.

The second critical feature was that in the course of the debate Lord Woolf, lord chief justice, announced he had changed his view and was now in favour of a supreme court. He urged the House to vote in favour of the Bill. Inevitably a course supported by the senior lord of appeal, the lord chief justice and half the lords of appeal was likely to be attractive to peers with no legal expertise of their own.

The government won the crucial division by 199 votes to 133. As the headline in the next day's *Guardian* put it, 'About-turn by Woolf saves supreme court.'

The Constitutional Reform Act was enacted in 2005. Adaptation of the existing building took some years, and the Queen officially opened the Supreme Court of the United Kingdom on 16th October 2009. The site chosen was in an appropriately symbolic location on Parliament Square, with the judiciary, the legislature, the executive (the treasury) and the established church on the four sides.

Law lords in committee room in 2005: (standing) Lords Walker, Carswell, Baroness Hale, Brown, Rodger, Hope, Scott, Saville, Hoffmann (seated) Nicholls, Bingham and Steyn.

Come Out Into The Sun

CHAPTER 31

A Change Of Scene
Holidays

THIS IS A difficult chapter to write and I was inclined to omit it altogether. Most accounts of other people's holiday activities, covering a period as short as a year, are boring. A blow-by-blow history of holidays taken over fifty years would surely be insufferable.

On reflection I decided that would be weak-minded. The summer holidays meant much to Jenny and me and the children. They were a feature of our lives, a highlight of the year. To leave them unmentioned even in outline would make these reminiscences incomplete. Overall they are part of our joint family memory, an optional extra for readers.

In 1961, our first year of marriage, we flew to Jersey and cycled energetically around parts of the island, alongside the rows of ripening tomatoes. For the next few years we stayed with family, as our holidays became more curtailed by Jenny expecting and having our first two babies.

In 1966, when John was nearly three and Gill nearly one, we spread our wings just a little by driving to north Cornwall and staying in a cottage at Port Gaverne, a small seaside village. This journey revealed all too vividly that John was not a good car traveller. We resolved that in future we would holiday more locally.

For the next three years we stayed at the seaside house of Mick and Patricia Prichard in Angmering-on-Sea, Sussex. Patricia was Christopher's godmother, and Mick's brother Michael had supervised Jenny in Roman law when she was at Girton. This was a quiet place and suited us admirably.

As the children grew up they needed playmates and access to a sandy beach. In 1970 we switched our allegiance to a children's hotel in Swanage, Dorset, located close to the beach and with an indoor swimming pool. One particularly attractive feature was that we had a set of bedrooms behind a single door opening onto the hotel corridor. For the children the beach was the top priority, but we made trips to Corfe Castle and Poole Harbour and explored the local headlands. We holidayed there for five years. Except for the first year the weather each summer was ideal.

By 1975 we were in need of a change. The choice fell on the Isle of Wight, having the added interest of sailing across the Solent. For the next two years we stayed in Freshwater, at the western corner of the island. For forty years our hotel, Farringford House, had been the much loved home of Lord Tennyson until his death in 1892. He was the poet laureate during most of Queen Victoria's reign, in succession to William Wordsworth who died in 1850. Tennyson's was the longest tenure of any poet laureate before or since.

The house was very evocative, with a Tennyson library and other reminders of him. The children slept in the room which had been his study and where he is said to have written the poem 'Maud' ('Come into the garden, Maud…'). At the foot of the hotel garden a gate led directly onto the chalk down, now known as Tennyson Down. Tennyson wrote:

'Where, far from noise and smoke of town
I watch the twilight falling brown,
All round a careless-ordered garden,
Close to the ridge of a noble down.'

A long line of mature elm trees sheltered one side of the entrance drive. The familiar words, 'the moan of doves in immemorial elms, and murmuring of innumerable bees', were written by Tennyson in 1870 when he lived in this house. The trees we saw were, surely, the very elms he had in mind. When we returned the following year the doves were still there. So were the trees, but they were dead. They had succumbed to Dutch elm disease.

The island was full of interest. We walked along Tennyson Down to the Needles stacks; the children enjoyed the sandy beach of Freshwater Bay and building a model dinosaur they have never forgotten. The lift down to Alum Bay with its striped sands in the cliff was another excitement. A few miles along the coast was Blackgang Chine, a dramatic coastal ravine, since destroyed by frequent landslides, with life-sized pirate ships and fairy lights at night. Further afield were Carisbrooke castle, where Charles I was imprisoned, and Osborne House.

Then we decided it was time for the children to see something of Scotland. In 1977 we put the car on the 'sleeper' train to Inverness. From there we explored the west coast, culminating in the Highland games in Portree on the Isle of Skye. We were intrigued to note that the shops displayed their goods with the prices in German.

The following year we tried our hands at a holiday in France. We booked a villa at Erquy, a small village in northern Brittany, within reach of the sea. We were much disturbed in March when a large oil tanker, *Amoco Cadiz*, ran aground off the coast of Brittany, resulting in its entire cargo of oil and fuel oil being spilled into the sea. This was the largest oil spill of its kind in history up to that date. The oil was spread along forty-five miles of the French shoreline. More than 20,000 sea birds died.

The summer of 1978 proved to be cold and wet. By the time August arrived we were in two minds over whether it was worth going to Brittany. Somewhat apprehensively, we went.

We were extremely fortunate. Even the channel crossing to St-Malo was gentle. As we expected, the beaches were empty but, contrary to what we feared, we came across no oil at all. The Sables d'Or were truly golden and the weather was simply glorious every day from dawn to dusk, with brilliant sunsets. The highlight of the visit was when I parked the car on the sloping sides of the causeway leading to le Mont St Michel and we all hoped I had understood the French tidal charts.

In 1979 we went north to Grange-over-Sands and then on to the Lake District, near Keswick. This was another wet summer, so wet that we could only glimpse Furness Abbey through the closed windows of the car. We left the croquet lawn at the first hotel in a dreadful mess. The hotelier at the Keswick hotel, the Red House hotel, was more prudent and would not let us use his croquet lawn. John and I scrambled up Skiddaw but, much to Christopher's disappointment, he was told he was too young to join us. This rebuff did not discourage him. Indeed, it may have had the opposite effect, because in later life he became an enthusiastic walker and mountaineer, trekking and climbing all over the world, including Mont Blanc and other dangerous mountains.

On our return journey we called on Gaynor in Stepping Hill and Brandon and Mary Jackson in Bradford. While we were visiting Haworth news broke that the Irish Republican Army had blown up Earl Mountbatten, another unforgettable moment.

All three children, independently of each other, have specifically reminded me of an occasion at the Red House hotel which, erroneously in my view, they describe as 'Daddy's tantrum'. So I have to mention this incident with, of course, the utmost objectivity. The day John and I walked up Skiddaw was the only fine day in the whole week. Every other day was cold and wet and miserable. One evening we went into dinner in the hotel dining room cold and hungry. When we reached the pudding stage the waitress told us that the hot pudding on the menu was now 'off' and all that remained available was ice cream. I thought this was a poor show, and said so, and asked to see the manager. I was invited to leave the table and go to his office. I declined, and said the manager should come to the table. After a pause, and with no sign of the manager, the waitress returned and asked whether some hot pancakes would do. 'Yes', I said, 'that would be fine.' But by the time they were cooked and brought to the table the children's appetites had fled because, as they said, they were so embarrassed by their father's behaviour. All they wanted now was ice cream. With some encouragement they ate the pancakes. The moral of this story? I do not know.

For the next three years we holidayed principally in Devon and Cornwall, partly at the Mill End hotel at Chagford, on the edge of Dartmoor, and partly at another holiday house belonging to Mick and Pat Prichard. Their house was splendidly sited overlooking Bude bay. Now that the children were growing up we walked further. The coast of north Cornwall is particularly attractive, even if hard work when going up and down along the cliffs. I was always keen to look inside any old churches near our routes. The children restricted me to ten churches on each holiday, a cathedral counting as two. Around these holiday breaks we fitted in days in Bath, very popular with the children, and our first visit to Paris.

In 1983 we went on our first cruise, with the Swan Hellenic line. This was a great adventure. We were new to the Mediterranean, and every port of call was exciting. The curtain raiser was spectacular, sailing from the quay at Venice and looking across at St Mark's Square in the setting sun, always an uplifting sight. The ship followed what was in those days a typical Swan Hellenic route: down the Adriatic, Corfu, Delphi (with its numinous atmosphere), Athens, Delos, Rhodes, through the Aegean sea, Troy, Dardanelles and Gallipoli to Istanbul and a first sight of the magnificent basilica of Hagia Sophia (now a museum) and the 'blue' Sultan Ahmed mosque. This was a memorable visit to a mosque, an occasion the children have never forgotten. Then back to Venice in time to have a day to explore that remarkable city. In Split the locals were unwilling to serve us. They thought we were Germans.

Christopher, aged twelve, was so captivated by everything that throughout his first term at Winchester he followed the route of Orpheus on a map pinned up in his room. Thus was he bitten by the travelling bug.

That was 1983. Over the next five years we explored parts of Austria, with Vienna and Salzburg high on the list, the Italian lakes of Maggiore and Garda, Florence, and a quick visit to Switzerland and the Matterhorn where we were surprised to see how much snow had fallen at a low height as early as August. In 1987 we had an interlude in south Wales, and Jenny and I made our first visit to Rome.

By the summer of 1989 the children were emancipated as far as summer holidays were concerned. This was the first year we travelled alone although Christopher, also touring Italy on his own, joined us briefly on two occasions. We went on a fortnight's coach tour of the art treasures of the hill towns of Italy, run by Swan Hellenic. Even now the roll call of these towns makes me tingle: Arezzo, Urbino, Gubbio, Perugia,

On the path to Rome: Oliver Mayo explaining the subtleties of maize heads.

Montefalco, Assisi, Spello, Spoleto, Orvieto, Cortona, San Gimignano. Christopher joined the party for an evening in Siena. We saw many wonderful pictures and frescos by Piero della Francesca, Uccello, Raphael, Pinturicchio, Signorelli, Perugino, Filippo Lippi and others. But it was a coach tour, and at one stop when we alighted from the coach we gazed longingly at the surrounding hillsides and wished we could walk over them. As I shall explain in a moment, this sentiment was to change the shape of our summers for over ten years.

In 1990 Jenny and I went to the northeast of England: Fountains Abbey and then on to Holy Island, walking along the beach to Bamburgh and Seahouses and on the moors inland from Alnwick. Then we ventured to Spain for a few days at Granada, where we joined Christopher in enjoying the Alhambra. He made us get up early so we could absorb the tranquillity of the Cour des Lions and the gardens of the Generalife.

In February 1991 I gave a lecture: 'Keeping the civil law up to date: flexibility and certainty in the 1990s' at University College London in its series of Current

Legal Problems. At dinner afterwards Jenny sat next to Jacqueline Dyson, dean of the college. They fell into talking about holidays. Jenny mentioned how much we enjoyed Italy but were sorry there seemed to be no way we could walk in the lovely countryside. The upshot was that Jacqueline introduced us to Alternative Travel Group, a company which organised small guided walking groups in Italy and elsewhere but did not advertise. Having seen its brochure we booked places on the 'Unknown Umbria' trip.

Our enjoyment of this trip is evident from the fact that, save for one year when we visited India, we holidayed with this group continually for more than ten years. We liked the exercise in the fresh air in all weathers and seeing interesting places in Italy, principally in Tuscany and Umbria, as well as in Spain and France. Our companions varied but nearly all were friendly and kind and interesting. Most were English, but over the years there was a sprinkling from many parts of the world. A minibus carried our luggage from place to place, and each day the tour manager produced a cold lunch of local produce. The tour leader accompanied us on our walks which varied in ease and difficulty. Typically we walked between ten and fifteen miles each day, sometimes more.

The overall length of the trips also varied. Most lasted a week but we preferred the longer treks. My two favourite walks were the longest. Top of the list was the 150-mile walk from Siena to Rome. In order to be fit enough to enjoy these walks we prepared ourselves in advance by tramping in our walking boots around Surrey and Sussex for a distance equal to that of our forthcoming holiday. So after our 'Path to Rome' trip we had walked 300 miles. We were fit.

This trip lasted most of a fortnight. We set out from Siena through its medieval gates as the sun was rising; we paused by the Benedictine abbey of Sant'Antimo and listened to the monks' plainchant; we climbed the slopes of Monte Amiata in pouring rain and at the top consumed some welcome hot soup; we lingered for two days beside Lake Bolsena; we walked into Montefiascone along the ancient Via Cassia; we meandered through hazelnut groves where the farmers' machinery made a fearsome noise gathering up the nuts. We marched into Rome across the Ponte Flamino and along the Tiber, reciting aloud what we could remember of Lord Macaulay's tale of Horatius ('Lars Porsena of Clusium…') until we reached St Peter's, tired but triumphant. And there was time to have another look at Michelangelo's Pieta, that most beautiful of sculptures.

Another excellent trip was the fifteen-day Camino de Santiago. We walked selected portions of the old pilgrimage route from St-Jean-Pied-de-Port to Santiago de Compostela. We had a tough first day, climbing from sea level up and over the

Pyrenees and down into Spain at the monastery of Roncesvalles. We then followed as much of the path of the ancient Camino as had not been absorbed into a modern road. We passed through Pamplona but no bulls were on the loose in the streets. We spent nights in Burgos and Leon, both with magnificent cathedrals. Once when Jenny paused to change her socks at the side of the road a newspaper company stopped to record this event on film, but we never saw the results.

As we proceeded further west into Galicia the weather deteriorated. On a day of torrential rain we lunched at a restaurant and were fed on octopus, before reaching Astorga with a splendid view of Gaudí's Bishop's palace. I nearly jumped out of my skin when I put some money into a slot inside the church to bring on the lights and at the same moment the organ beside me started playing loudly.

Gradually the pilgrimage milestones became more frequent and more prominent. There was an increasing sense of excitement in the air. When we marched through the villages and set the dogs barking the cottagers came to their doors and wished us 'buen camino' and offered us the traditional homemade sweetmeats. We passed the stream where pilgrims washed their clothes as they approached Santiago but we were too wet to indulge in this historic custom. When we reached Santiago we did follow the custom of going straight to the cathedral and embracing the statue of St James above the altar. We had walked 130 miles, not as far as the early pilgrims but still a goodly way. We were presented with a brass scallop shell, the emblem of St James, worn by pilgrims.

Our last walk with ATG was in Sicily in 2004. Jenny had been having trouble with one of her hips for some time. In 2005 we began our next phase of summer holidays. From 2005 we went on a summer cruise each year for the next nine years, save for 2006 when Jenny was recovering from having a hip replacement. For two years we cruised on *Hebridean Princess*, a small but comfortable ship, until the company went bust. Otherwise with our old friend Swan Hellenic but now taken over by new owners. Mostly we sailed in the Mediterranean plus trips around the Black Sea, through the Baltic to St Petersburg, and down the French Atlantic coast. Neither of us is a good sailor, and it was on this French trip that we met a force eight gale in the Bay of Biscay, the worst storm we encountered on all our cruises.

Of our many wonderful experiences we particularly enjoyed the outstanding fine art collections and places replete with history: the art galleries in Amsterdam, the temples in Sicily, the Syrian Krak des Chevaliers (before it was damaged recently), the site of the charge of the Light Brigade in the Crimea, Petra, the pyramids, Luxor and the valley of the kings.

We delighted in all these, but top of our list was St Catherine's monastery at the foot of Mount Sinai. This monastery, miles from anywhere, was built by Emperor Justinian in the 6th century with thick and powerful walls to defend the monks from attacks by marauding Saracens. It is the oldest continuously inhabited monastery in the Christian world. Justinian presented to the monastery 200 Egyptians and 200 Wallachians to serve the monks as serfs. Within the walls a church was built for the monks and a mosque for the Muslim servants.

Over the centuries the monastery built up an impressive collection of icons and manuscripts, preserved largely by its isolation. In the mid-19th century a German biblical scholar Constantin von Tischendorf made several visits to the monastery. He made his last visit in 1859, this time with the patronage of the Tsar of Russia Alexander II, the most powerful man in the whole of Orthodox Christiandom. He was shown a parcel of more than 300 parchments, containing the whole Bible. These parchments, since known as the codex Sinaiticus, were written in the 4th century, sometime between 325 and 360. They are the oldest surviving Bible containing the complete New Testament.

Tischendorf persuaded the monks to let him take the manuscripts to Russia in order to produce a published facsimile of the whole. He carried them to St Petersburg and presented them to the tsar. After the Russian revolution the Soviets' financial problems caused them to sell many of their precious manuscripts. In 1933 the British government bought the codex Sinaiticus for £100,000. When the manuscripts arrived in London they were taken to the British Museum. All the men in the crowds lining the roads took off their hats.

On our return to England Jenny and I traced the manuscripts to the British Library in London. In a darkened room we gazed at this remarkable piece of history.

I add a footnote. Tischendorf was disappointed with what he had found. In the codex Sinaiticus Mark's gospel does not contain the last twelve verses. This is a major omission because these are the only verses in that gospel which describe Jesus' resurrection appearances. A similar omission appears in other early manuscripts of Mark's gospel, such as the codex Vaticanus. This has given rise to a much debated conundrum. Since Mark's account seems to be the earliest of the three synoptic gospels, and his account seems to be the basis of the accounts of Matthew and Luke, on what did Matthew, Luke and John base their accounts of Jesus' resurrection?

I should now return to the summer of 1992 when we laid aside walking in favour of accompanying John and Divya to India. The entire trip was most beautifully planned by Vinoo Ubhayakar, a longstanding friend of the Bhatia family. We were thoroughly spoilt, from the very beginning.

Jenny in the pyramids.

We started in the Taj Mahal hotel in Bombay (Mumbai) beside the Gateway to India. We relaxed at the Bombay Gymkhana, founded in 1875, and at the home of Divya's parents Ushi and Raj Bhatia. He was an Air India pilot of some distinction, flying Mrs Gandhi all over the world. We visited famous landmarks such as the railway station, and walked to the 'Afghan church' whose steeple greets those entering the harbour. The church pews had slots to hold rifles. The church commemorates several thousand soldiers who died in the first and second Afghan wars during the Great Game. 'Afghanistan': do we never learn?

From Bombay the next stop was Udaipur, where we stayed at the ornate Lake Palace hotel in the middle of the lake. One evening we had drinks with the Maharana, Arvind Singh Mewar, in his palace on the edge of the lake. When the electric lighting failed we continued talking in the dark for several minutes as though nothing had happened and without any mention when the lights returned.

In Jodhpur we stayed in what had been a vast, rather austere palace with elaborate architecture. The buildings in the valley below the fort were painted blue to repel the heat of the sun. The entrance portals of the fort were covered in poignant handprints affixed there by wives as they walked out to be burned alive on their husband's funeral pyre.

In this part of India, so we were told, there was very little rain, if any. Whilst we were there it rained so heavily we could not go out, and the rain delayed for a day the flight of the aeroplane taking us on to Jaipur. In Jaipur, the 'pink city' of India, we stayed at the Rambagh Palace with its magnificent grounds abounding in monkeys, and visited the Palace of the Winds. Inevitably we drove out to Amber for an elephant ride up to the Amber Fort. And then on to Agra and the Taj Mahal, pausing on the way for a quick look (in heavy rain) at the red sandstone city of Fatehpur Sikri.

Delhi was the end of our journey in India, where we visited the Red Fort and could not fail to notice Lutyens' buildings in 'New Delhi'. Here we had some very happy visits to family members. John and I hailed a scooter. At the hotel the driver had to stop outside the hotel driveway as the hotel would not permit the entry of such a modest vehicle.

At this stage we parted company from John and Divya. Jenny and I went on a frolic of our own to Nepal for a few days. Kathmandu, since devastated by a series of earthquakes, was a fascinating place, full of smiling people but still living in an undeveloped world of its own. I was hoping to see something of the Himalayas, and so we flew further north to Pokhara.

The airport at Pokhara was the most primitive I have ever used. A public footpath crossed the landing strip. When a plane was due to land a whistle was blown to alert the local populace not to use the footpath until the plane had landed.

We stayed at Fishtail Lodge in the middle of a lake. Until now we had gone vegetarian on our Indian trip because we had been warned about the risk of eating hotel meat. By now our digestive systems had started to rebel against the constant spicy food, so we risked all and had some local fish, without ill effects.

Early each morning I went outside in the hope of a glimpse of the distant mountain ranges, without success until our last day. Then the mists had lifted and the morning sky was clear. Some way above the horizon and stretching its entire length I saw, indeed I could not fail to see, what seemed to be a broad band of thick white cloud. To English eyes a storm was brewing. Not so. It took me a while to realise I was looking at distant snow, not cloud, up to an amazing height. It was a wonderful sight.

In later years, in addition to our summer holidays, Jenny and I had a winter break at Cobblers Cove in Barbados and a spring break at the Old Rectory at Great

Snoring, Norfolk. In Norfolk we walked on the beaches and investigated some of the many marvellous churches. Unlike the children Jenny imposed no ceiling on the number of churches I could visit during each holiday.

We also lodged with our children. In 2001, very bravely for us, we hired a car in France and stayed several nights with John and family at their farmhouse in the Vendée. We then explored some of the chateaux in the Loire valley.

We have also holidayed, more than once, at Christopher's thatched cottage in the Cotswolds, at Great Tew, and enjoyed many marvellous Christmas festivities with Gill and Stephen at their lovely home in Ockley with all other family members who could come.

CHAPTER 32

Deus Nobis Haec Otia Fecit
In the Garden

HOLIDAYS APART AND however busy, everyone needs some form of relaxation which is readily available. Over the years tending my garden has been for me a great source of peace and relaxation, hence enjoyment. The contrast between this activity and my daily round could hardly have been more complete. Unlike the Bar and the judicial bench this was physical work, done out-of-doors, and without any time pressure. I confess the lack of pressure owed much to always having help with the heavy work, help which gradually increased in extent over the years.

A sad feature of the garden, common throughout much of the country, has been the decline in the number of songbirds and, with this, the almost total absence of a dawn chorus. The silent spring, indeed. In recent years blackbirds have been our sole songsters. Once numerous but now never seen in my garden are thrushes, sparrows, starlings, chaffinches, bullfinches, goldcrests, woodpeckers, treecreepers, even jays. At one time there were enough birds for Gill to make a bird map of the garden. It is many years now since I heard a cuckoo, formerly a regular harbinger of late spring. For some years a cuckoo called from our wood. One morning Gill responded in kind and we never heard or saw him again. We were left to ponder whether he feared a rival, or was upset by her mimicry of his advertising call, or there was simply no connection.

Blackbirds and tits are still faithful residents, as is the occasional wren. Robins remain, and supervise me closely whenever I do anything in the flower beds. Otherwise magpies, crows, and pigeons have taken over. They don't sing and they are far more destructive, especially with my lawns. Our most recent visitors, raiders but not residents, are parakeets with their long pointed tails. Despite their attractive lime-green plumage, their appetite for buds on the blossom of fruit trees makes them unwelcome guests. The grey squirrels still live here. They, and the magpies, studiously ignore each other. At night the urban foxes set off the security lights.

In the winter, apart from table tennis and darts in the garage, snow was the only outside excitement for the children. They always built a snowman. One year John and his cousin Timothy went to America and toured extensively on Greyhound

The house at Cobham.

coaches. Before he left home John traced 'Q P R' in large letters in the snow, and when he returned the letters were still there. So was the snowman, although minus his carrot nose and coal eyes. John still supports Queens Park Rangers, in the same way as I have faithfully followed the fortunes of Tranmere Rovers in Birkenhead. My camera, which he had borrowed, froze up at Niagara Falls and was never usable again.

In the summer the garden was, effectively, an additional room. During his weekends in Winchester Christopher fashioned a splendid outdoor table, which we still use for meals and drinks. The garden functioned, even more, as a playground. To the children it was irresistible, at all ages. The first stage was a double swing I bought in 1969 at Gamages, then a well-known store at Holborn Circus, within easy reach of Lincoln's Inn. The idea of this swing, preventing quarrels, came from the children falling in love with a similar swing in Michael Rich's garden in Dulwich. This swing has served two generations and is still in good shape.

The next step was hide-and-seek. For this the layout of the garden was ideal, with its several different sections divided by hornbeam and yew hedges. Tricycles

The garden, in winter…

…late spring…

and bicycles followed and, later, as the children grew up, football and badminton and cricket became the vogue, with the local rule that 'if you hit the ball into a flower bed you are out.' Ultimately croquet took over. The undulations in the lawn gave a marked advantage to home players over visitors.

When John and a local friend kicked a football at each other a neighbour's dog Dandy always sat and watched, fascinated, through a gap in the hedge. Only once did he come into the garden, and that was when Gill fell off her bicycle with a loud shriek and he ran to her side. When she had struggled to her feet again he returned to his accustomed spot.

A cat Jassy, belonging to the neighbour on the other side of the garden, often came in and fell asleep in the greenhouse. When she emerged, stupefied from the heat, she would join in a game of croquet, lying down on her back, quite immovably, in front of one of the hoops.

Gradually I abandoned growing fruit and vegetables. The light sandy soil was far from ideal. Small birds got trapped in the fruit cage, and extricating them from the netting and repairing the damage year after year became irksome. The peas were fine but not plentiful; the broad beans were invariably covered in black fly; the carrots also attracted fly and seldom prospered, and Jenny said it was easier to buy new potatoes from Waitrose than to dig them up. In the winter the pigeons feasted on the brassica and, when they had consumed all those leaves, they turned to the spinach and did the same again. Rhubarb did well, as did runner beans, but this seemed a small return for a lot of work. So they were all replaced by grass and shrubs.

One summer I fell off a ladder and broke some ribs while picking greengages from a fruit tree. Jenny was so determined it would not happen again that the tree had to be cut down, as though my accident was the fault of the tree. The apple trees remain, of which Worcester Permain and Bramleys are the best, but I am banned from climbing ladders.

When Christopher was about six years old Jenny and I went to choose a garden ornament of about his height. He came with us as our measuring stick. Using him in this way we acquired a stone statue of a young Pan-like figure, playing cymbals rather than the reed pipes associated with him as an adult. In a way this is the focal point of the garden.

...early summer and the first roses...

...and the roses at their best.

CHAPTER 33

Family
Past and Present

I MUST NOW mention what had been happening elsewhere in the family. Mum and Dad enjoyed many happy years together in Cornwall. Mum was wont to say these were the happiest days of her life. This is where Marjorie and Joyce went to school. University followed, with Marjorie at Goldsmiths' College in London and Joyce at Newcastle. Some time after they had both married and set up their own homes Mum and my father decided to move nearer their daughters. For several years they lived in Swanage, in a house towards the top end of a steep road leading out of the centre of the town. The house had three floors but no garden. Here they also gave a home to Mum's sister Jessie for a number of years.

When this tall building no longer suited them they moved again, this time to a bungalow in the quiet village of Verwood, Dorset. My father rejoiced in having a garden once more. Joyce settled Jessie in a Church of England home and continued to see her for the rest of her life.

For a long time my father suffered from diabetes. In 1992 they decided to share a home with Joy and her husband Tony. One day before the move was completed and after not having met for many years, Dad's sister called to see him. That very night he died, aged ninety-one.

So Mum alone moved into the happily named Peace Cottage at Tiptoe, near Lymington, Hampshire, with Joy and 'Anton' Bingham, as she insisted on calling Joy's husband because she did not care for the name Tony. As Mum's health deteriorated they both nursed her with sustained love and care. To do this Joy gave up her job as a care homes inspector. Marjorie visited every week. In 2007 Mum died at the ripe age of ninety-seven years.

Marjorie lived not too far away, in Bowerchalke, Wiltshire. Her husband Stephen had set up his own business of designing and manufacturing electronic control panels in Blandford, Dorset, under the name Sarum Electronics Ltd. He ran this business until he retired towards the end of 2014. They had two children, Hugh and Catherine. Catherine, who was Gill's bridesmaid in 1990, married Jamie Gosling.

Family on Mum's 90th birthday.

They also lived in Bowerchalke. Hugh had a brilliant university career in engineering, obtaining a first at Loughborough and then an MSc at Imperial College, London.

The year 2010 was our own annus horribilis. Jenny's sister Gaynor died in late June, followed by Ushi's husband Rajindar (known universally as Raj) shortly before Christmas. Gay was Jenny's closest friend and a much loved member of the family. She came and stayed with us in Cobham several times a year. Without her, Christmas would have been incomplete. Raj was very much part of the life of Divya and John and their family because he lived nearby. He endeared himself to all he met, young and old. Then at Easter in the following year Clifford died, a few days short of his eightieth birthday. For some years he was incapacitated increasingly by Parkinson's disease. I never heard him complain. Joan nursed him devotedly at home.

My six grandchildren, to bring the family picture up to date, span eleven years spreading downwards from Tom, currently aged twenty. At the time of writing Tom is in his second year reading law at Trinity Hall, and Ayesha is waiting to take up her place in October to read modern languages at Sidney Sussex College, Cambridge. Edward is in the sixth form at Charterhouse. Charlie will be taking his GCSEs next year at Seaford. Florence is about to start at Wimbledon High School and Henry is a pupil at King's College Junior School, Wimbledon.

Family

Family at home celebrating our golden wedding anniversary.

CHAPTER 34

Time To Stop
Retirement: 2007

LORD GOFF, A great judge, was always concerned that his judgments should be founded on legal principles. Lord Cooke, another great judge, attached much store to simplicity. I agreed with them both. A third ingredient, to which I attached importance, is brevity. The drawback of this self-imposed writing style is that it can add appreciably to the time taken in drafting a complicated document. Every draftsman knows it is easier to write a long document than a short one.

By October 2006 I was beginning to feel the physical strain imposed by full-time work as a lord of appeal, in particular the non-stop demands of judgment writing. I had been a lord of appeal for twelve years, five of them as the second senior lord of appeal. At the end of the month I decided it was time to stop. Having told Tom Bingham of my intention I wrote to the lord chancellor, Charlie Falconer, a letter of resignation as from January 2007. He sent me this generous hand-written reply:

'I am profoundly saddened that you are retiring. There are a few judges in a generation who significantly affect the development of the law. You unquestionably have been one of them. Throughout the whole of your judicial career you have been both an innovator and a profound explainer of the law. I suspect success as the former depends entirely upon being the latter.

Your peers hold you in the highest possible regard. I have not spoken to any of them since receiving your letter. But I have no doubt that they will feel they have lost one of their greatest talents.

Although there are matters on which we have disagreed, you have been an utter delight to deal with.

It was good to glimpse you at the silk ceremony when John took silk. As we lose one Nicholls we gain (or at least get closer to gaining) another.

The 10th January is very close. You leave at a peak. I hope we can persuade you to continue to sit in a range of capacities.

Your loss is incalculable.'

I received several very kind letters. Not without some hyperbole one described my contribution to the law as 'monumental'. Another said my judgments were of 'outstanding quality'. I will quote in full just one other letter, from Igor Judge, the lord chief justice from 2008:

> 'I can only say it once more – but I am very sorry you are retiring. Every judicial member of the House of Lords is an ornament, but not all are blessed with your clarity of vision, your insights into long term consequences, or your ability to explain it all to those of us who like our law to be simple. You will be greatly missed by us all.'

Each year the lords of appeal held a private dinner with their wives at one of the Inns of Courts or some other suitably discreet venue such as the Athenaeum club in Pall Mall. The practice was that they invited as their guests any lord of appeal, plus spouse, who had retired during the year. I expected that Jenny and I would be accorded a like invitation after my retirement and, indeed, we were.

To my surprise the lord chancellor on behalf of the government invited Jenny and me and all the children to a dinner at Lancaster House. Lancaster House is a magnificent building, close to St James's palace, used for government functions. This was a singular honour not previously conferred on a lord of appeal. Although he would never admit it, I have no doubt this invitation was instigated by Tom Bingham.

At the last minute the arrangements altered. On the very day the dinner was due to be held there was a change of lord chancellor. Charlie Falconer was replaced by Jack Straw. Both attended the dinner, together with Derry Irvine, a former lord chancellor. This meant that no fewer than three lord chancellors were present.

The dinner was a splendid occasion in a very special setting. All three children and their spouses attended and there was a goodly turn out of lords of appeal together, in each case, with wife or husband.

After the dinner Charlie Falconer wrote again, saying the dinner was a privilege he was very keen not to miss. He added: 'You have contributed so much to the law. It was right that three Lord Chancellors came to pay their respects.'

Harry Woolf, Tom Bingham and I were all born in the same year. By 2007 Harry had already retired from the office of lord chief justice. His work was celebrated with a dinner in Lancaster House, at which Jenny and I were present. I was particularly pleased that in 2008 a like dinner was held for Tom on his retirement from being senior lord of appeal on reaching the compulsory retirement age of seventy-five years. Jenny and I attended what was quite a riotous evening. His children had arranged for a brass band to attend, for us all to join in singing suitably laudatory songs at the end of the meal.

These three dinners were a wonderful climax for the 1933 contingent.

CHAPTER 35

Eighty Years
Cliveden: January 2013

I CELEBRATED MY eightieth birthday by inviting immediate family to Cliveden House, Berkshire, for the weekend. This is a stately building with an interesting history, set in beautiful grounds maintained by the National Trust. Everyone was able to come, and there were no last minute crises. It is not always easy for children to escape from boarding school during term time but somehow Tom and Ayesha managed.

At Cliveden there was something for every age group. The snow cleared quickly and did not obstruct the family members who must kick a football at every opportunity. Nor did it hinder those who chose to stroll round the parterre and step gingerly down to the river Thames. Charlie helped Ushi back up the slippery slope, and Edward gave Florence a piggy-back ride over a prolonged distance. She loved it but it nearly finished him off for the rest of the day.

The indoor swimming pool was heated; the indoor tennis court was the first constructed in this country. There was a snooker table in the basement for those not content simply to sit before a blazing fire in the marvellous hall lined with excellent portraits. Our period bedrooms bore names evocative of the colourful history of the house: Westminster, Lady Astor, Lord Gibson, T E Lawrence, Barry, Warrender. Christopher gave me a customised version of the game of Monopoly which was fun to play with Florence and Henry.

Jenny and I had chosen menus in advance for the evening meals, offering a wide range of choice. We dined as a family by ourselves in the charming boudoir room. The food, wine and service were all excellent. At dinner on Friday evening, which was my actual birthday, John addressed me with a poem he had composed for the occasion. It summarises my eighty years in eighty words:

'First a son and brother, then at six a new mother;
Birkenhead school – you thrive;
Two sisters arrive;
Liverpool and Cambridge – stellar, then the Bar;
Jennifer met, married, your lifelong love.

To Meadows and two kids,
To Little Blakeney and a third;
QC to Judge, LJ,V-C, Lord of Appeal;
In the absence of Latin,
"Let Equity Prevail"!

Treasurer, Fellow, President – honours abound;
Today, your family – six-grandchildren – you surround
What more to say,
Simply, Happy Birthday!'

I could not have wished for a happier birthday.

At Cliveden – the boys...

…and the girls.

CHAPTER 36

Looking Back
2015

EVERY BIOGRAPHY IS selective. An autobiography is selective and also unreliable, whether overstated or understated. We cannot see ourselves as others see us. We cannot remember, or perhaps never knew, the effect of our acts or omissions on others. So why write this selective and unreliable account at all? Is it no more than self-indulgence, satisfying a desire for self-glorification?

I think not. In times to come there may be those who wish they had known more about me. I wish I had known more about my mother. This is not an adverse reflection on Mum's upbringing of two boys, who were not her own, in the absence of their father in difficult conditions. But I share some of my mother's genes. It seems to me wholly natural and proper to wish to know something of her life, her family, her childhood, her education, her beliefs and interests. In the foregoing pages I have sought to record about myself something of what I wish I had known about her.

I have led a very fortunate life. Of that I am profoundly aware. Chance has played a part, as always. More importantly, every step taken by me owes much to the kindness and support of others. I like to think I too have helped others whenever possible but that I cannot judge. Certainly I fear that any help I have given does not stand comparison with what I have received.

I have spent my life in the law. I must mention two lawyers, both judges but very different personalities, whose work I have most admired. The first is Lord Denning.

Lord Denning lived to be 100. At his memorial service in Westminster Abbey Lord Bingham said he was 'the best-known and best-loved judge in our history'. In his contribution to the *Oxford Dictionary of National Biography* Lord Goff described him as the greatest English judge of the 20th century.

The present generation of lawyers can be forgiven for not appreciating the profound influence Lord Denning had on the law half a century ago. In the middle of the last century the law was stagnant. Lord Devlin, himself a distinguished lord of appeal, wrote in 1984:

'The old-fashioned judge looked to the letter of the statute and for the case on all fours. He knew that he had to do justice according to law. Either he

Lord Denning, with walking stick, in procession from Westminster Abbey with (l to r) Lords Roskill, Brightman and Scarman.

assumed that the law when strictly applied would always do justice or else he decided that, if it did not, it was not his business to interfere. Today this is not the idea.'

This change in attitude was largely brought about single-handed by Lord Denning in the 1950s and 1960s. Change was desperately needed and he met this need. His contribution to the development of the law was immense. One of his campaigns, of enormous importance and ultimately successful, was to promote a purposive, rather than a literal, approach to the interpretation of documents and statutes.

He first hit the headlines with his decision in 1946 in the famous High Trees case. At that time he was a High Court judge. Two years later he moved to the Court of Appeal, and from then onwards Lord Justice Denning, or Lord Denning as he later became, was seldom out of the news. The law students, of whom I was one, loved him. He was hugely popular. They could understand his brief and lucid judgments; they admired the simplicity of his law and his determination to find or fashion a way to give effect to the 'merits' of a case. In their eyes he could do no wrong. He showed scant respect to decisions of the House of Lords by which, strictly, he was bound. When Viscount Simonds accused him of heresy in 1962 for abrogating old principles they applauded Lord Denning's iconoclasm and supported him, not the established order. In 1978 he reminded the attorney general that 'be you ever so high the law is above you,' and helped to lay the foundations for a rational and effective system of judicial review.

Lord Denning rejoiced in his reputation as a reformer and innovator. There was always a trickle of visitors into the back of his court to see the famous judge in action. When he addressed meetings of university undergraduates, which he did often, he enjoyed telling the story of the time a student wrote to him one Easter begging him not to give any more judgments before the students had taken their forthcoming exams because they could not keep pace with all his changes in the law.

When that generation of law students graduated and qualified as solicitors or barristers they carried with them Lord Denning's new, non-technical approach to the law. The transition was not altogether comfortable. If it is readily understandable that young newcomers should embrace new and appealing ideas with alacrity, it is equally understandable that those steeped in existing law and practices should be hesitant and doubtful. Established practitioners, and judges, were set in their ways and accustomed to the present state of the law and did not always welcome radical change. It took some time for the latest developments to be assimilated. More recently much the same happened when restitution was first introduced as a distinct cause of action.

While that slow process was taking place the outcome of cases was less predictable than usual. This made it difficult for lawyers to give firm advice to their clients. Even in Lord Denning's own court, where I appeared several times, the outcome was more difficult to forecast than normal. When I went into his court I was sure of only two matters: I would be treated courteously, which was not true of all the judges at that time, and if I had the 'merits' I started with a tremendous advantage. Conversely, if my client had no 'merits'.

Tom Denning had a brilliant mind and a remarkable memory coupled with an equally remarkable ability to deliver extempore judgments in the most complex cases. In almost all cases in his court he gave the first judgment. This could be embarrassing to his fellow lord justices. On one occasion in his court in a complicated case I took it for granted that the judges would take time to consider their judgments. Not so. At the conclusion of counsel's arguments Lord Denning turned at once to his colleague Lord Justice Bridge and, much to the latter's plainly evident surprise, asked, 'shall we deliver judgment now?' Lord Justice Bridge, looking a trifle embarrassed, said he would prefer to have more time to think before giving his judgment.

The judgments of Lord Denning are not cited as much now as in the last century. This is not an adverse reflection on his jurisprudence. Rather, the system has now accepted and absorbed his reforms and moved on from there.

Lord Wilberforce, a chancery lawyer, was an influence in my life at a later stage. He was another long-lived legal giant, dying at the age of ninety-five years. He sat in the House of Lords as a law lord for eighteen years from 1964. By then I was already in practice at the Bar.

Richard Wilberforce was a man of rare gifts. He had an exceptionally quick, incisive and independent mind. His analysis of underlying legal principles was invariably compelling, for he was also a man of vision. He was not given to wasting words, either in his judgments or elsewhere. Rather, he expressed himself with the simplicity and directness which betoken clear thinking. His approach to the law was rooted in abundant common sense and humanity.

On the few occasions his colleagues differed from him he used to say, engagingly, that this was due to deficiencies in presentation of the arguments by counsel. With all his gifts he remained modest and unassuming, always courteous and patient, of warm disposition but with a wry sense of humour.

Despite these qualities, or perhaps because of them, appearing as counsel before him could be an anxious experience. He had always read the papers in advance from cover to cover, and you were never sure what penetrating questions he might ask for which you were not prepared.

As a law lord he heard 465 appeals and gave individual judgments in very many of them. Therein lay his unique contribution to the development of the law. Whenever, as counsel or later as a judge, I had cause to look up a decision of the House of Lords in which he had participated I invariably turned first to his speech, assured of assistance. I never came away disappointed. I was never puzzled or unclear what it was he was trying to say. He was a model of clarity, always lucid even if, very rarely, I disagreed with his conclusion.

Turning to more personal matters, another feature of my life for which I am grateful is that Hector Hillaby, a member of 13 Old Square set of chambers, kindly put my name forward for election as a member of the Athenaeum Club, Pall Mall. I was duly elected in 1977. Ever since I have greatly enjoyed the amenities of this distinguished club and the opportunity to meet so many interesting people.

The club was founded in 1824. The front of the club house was decorated with a statue of Athena, the goddess of wisdom, together with a frieze which is a copy of the 'Elgin marbles' then recently rescued from the Parthenon in Athens. The erection of this frieze was controversial. When the third storey of the club house was being built as a later addition some members, in those pre-refrigeration days, would have preferred the available money to be spent on an ice house to provide cold storage in the summer rather than on this expensive decoration. The member in charge of this work was J W Croker, secretary to the admiralty, and he liked to get his own way. Hence the witticism:

'I'm John Wilson Croker,
I do as I please;
Instead of an ice house
I give you – a frieze!'

The first chairman of the club was Sir Humphrey Davy and Michael Faraday the first secretary. Over the years the club has a remarkable record of highly notable members. More than fifty of its members have won a Nobel Prize.

I have never been able to attend the club as much as I would have wished. The problem was the usual one: pressure of work and lack of time. When I was in practice in Lincoln's Inn and later on the bench in the law courts in the Strand, it was not easy to escape to Pall Mall. It was easier when I was based in the House of Lords, because the club was then within walking distance. For some years I was a member of the general committee, but when I was invited to be the chairman of the club I felt, with much regret, that I had to decline. I would not have had enough time to do the job properly.

Subsequently I served as one of the club's trustees, which was less demanding but very interesting because the trustees attended meetings of the general committee.

The club was founded as a 'gentleman's club'. With changing lifestyles the time came when the club needed to amend its rules to enable admission of women members. This gave rise to some controversy but, with surprisingly little ill-feeling and delay, the rules were changed in 2002.

The club, I have to say, has much improved from when I first joined. Now, the place is alive, with a warm and welcoming atmosphere. The food is better, the service is better, the décor is better, the club house is better attended. It is now, and has been for some years, an altogether excellent club. I feel privileged to have been a member.

I have enjoyed being able to maintain links with my school and universities although, to my regret, as one gets older visits to Merseyside are not so easy. I mention some recent events. I was delighted that in 2010 I was able to attend Chester cathedral and read a lesson at a service of commemoration and thanksgiving on the occasion of the sesquicentenary of the foundation of Birkenhead School. It was good to meet again two former headmasters and several past and present governors. It was a great pleasure in 2014 to have lunch with the chairman of the governors Andrew Sutton at his home and wish the outgoing headmaster John Clark well in his educational ventures in Nepal.

In January 2014 I joined many other Trinity Hall graduates in Cambridge in celebrating John Collier's eightieth birthday. This dinner took place in a temporary marquee in the front court of the college while the hall itself was being refurbished. On the following month I saw the newly refurbished hall in all its glory when I was invited to the annual dinner of the Trinity Hall legal society. I gave a talk on the topical subject of Human Rights and Sovereignty. Later in the year the Hall acquired a new master, Revd Dr Jeremy Morris, and I attended a welcoming dinner in London given by the college honorary fellows.

Events such as these, of which there were many, are always great fun, partly nostalgic, but also heartening to see how, half a century later, the current students are prospering in surroundings which were so familiar to me.

Music has played some part in my life, although not as much as I would have wished. I remember a piano in the house at Prenton but it was sold during the war. I do not recall it ever being played. So far as I know Mum did not play. My father played the organ but I never knew how that came about. I sometimes wondered whether my own mother was the original source of the piano.

So mine was not a musical family. Mum's sister Jean, who lived about a mile away, had a pianola. Several times I walked to her house and pedalled away at this strange instrument. I felt I was at least making music of a sort.

Then, apart from the orchestral visit to Birkenhead School already mentioned, I experienced a long musical gap until I became a student at Liverpool University in 1953. Borrowing '78' gramophone records of classical music was one of the facilities of the students' union, of which I made much use. In the early 1950s 78 rpm records were still the vogue, although listening to a symphony or concerto was seriously disjointed. Typically a 12-inch disc playing at a speed of seventy-eight revolutions per minute had a playing time of only four or five minutes per side. And mass-produced steel needles were short lived. A piece of music with a playing time of half an hour called for several changes of record, from one side of the disc to the other or from one disc to another, and a change of needle. I became so familiar with the stopping places in some pieces of music that for a long time whenever I heard this music again I expected a pause when those places were reached.

It is not surprising these records were replaced, initially by so-called long playing records (LPs), with three times as many grooves and revolving at the slower speed of 33 rpm and using a precision-made sapphire or diamond stylus. Their playing time was up to half an hour of recorded material per side. These were followed by the familiar compact discs and other improvements.

The Philharmonic Hall in Hope Street, Liverpool, was near the university, and students were permitted to attend final rehearsals free of charge. We could sit at the front of the stalls, which added to the interest and enjoyment. But these rehearsals had two drawbacks: they lacked the atmosphere of a proper performance and, more importantly, they suffered from the same defect as 78 records. Inevitably the performances were disjointed, as every now and then the conductor called a halt and required a repeat of a particular passage.

Very occasionally I bought a record for myself, but I remember the occasion when I decided that, given the choice between building a library of books and a collection of records, I opted for books. I could not afford both, and reprints of 'classical' literature were cheaper than records.

In later years I built up a small collection of records and discs of classical music and Italian opera, but the thought of learning to play a musical instrument never crossed my mind. Partly, I think, because I had grown accustomed to life without a piano, and partly also because buying a piano and having lessons, if I had thought of that at all, would have been way down my list of priorities.

As the years passed Jenny and I attended some opera at Covent Garden and Glyndebourne. There the matter rested until one day a few years ago, after I had retired from the bench, I suddenly thought, 'why not now?' in response to an unspoken regret I could not make music of my own. I had more time on my hands now than for many years.

With his customary generosity, Gill's husband Stephen, an accomplished player of several musical instruments, chose and bought a fine Roland keyboard for me.

Gill found a delightful teacher who quite understood I would not take any exams but just wished to play for my own pleasure. And so off I went, starting from scratch.

Playing has been fun, if hard going at times ('little and often'). I can manage some pieces, such as Beethoven's 'Fur Elise', if I learn the music more-or-less by heart. Then I enjoy my playing even if no one else does, although they are always too kind to say. Sometimes I have played on Stephen's grand piano, which makes a very different sound.

But I find I am still much too slow at reading a score and then translating this into the appropriate notes of the keyboard. More recently some of my fingers have reminded me they are happy typing on a computer but not accustomed to piano playing. Even so I am glad I started to learn, and I have not abandoned hope. This is unfinished business. As headmaster Bushell was wont to write laconically on my school reports: 'could do better'.

It is sad when people look back and wish their principal occupation had been different. I have no such regret. No doubt in part, perhaps in large part, this is because I was successful in my chosen profession. That always helps. Life at the Bar and on the bench was stimulating. Usually it was rewarding in the sense of intellectually satisfying and, as a barrister, in the financial sense as well. I worked alongside some exceptionally able colleagues. Almost all were delightful and congenial.

That is not to say the Bar, and indeed the judicial bench, have no snags. Every profession has drawbacks. The Bar is highly competitive and hence, as I found it, very time-demanding. The bench, at appellate level, was also time-demanding. I worked hard to the extent of having little time for leisure activities. That was a loss to me and to Jenny, especially in the early years of our marriage. That is a regret, but that was the price for the work I had chosen to do.

To me this and any other disadvantages weigh lightly in the scales when set against having an opportunity to share with others in bringing about improvements in the law, in helping to achieve a greater measure of fairness. *Aequitas praevaleat.*

And now for the garden…